SECRETS FROM MY FRENCH KITCHEN

SECRETS FROM MY FRENCH KITCHEN

FRANÇOISE BERNARD

MACDONALD & JANE'S · LONDON

First published in France in 1972 by
Librairie Hachette

Copyright © Françoise Bernard, 1972

This edition first published in Great Britain in 1977 by
Macdonald and Jane's Publishers Limited,
Paulton House, 8 Shepherdess Walk, London, N1

Copyright © Françoise Bernard, 1977
Illustrations Copyright © Macdonald and Jane's
Publishers Limited, 1977
ISBN 0 354 04085 5

Printed in Great Britain by
Redwood Burn Limited
Trowbridge & Esher

CONTENTS

FOREWORD	vi
INTRODUCTION	vii
STARTERS (APPETIZERS)	1
MAIN COURSE DISHES:	
MEAT	37
POULTRY AND GAME	101
FISH AND SHELLFISH	137
PASTA AND RICE	163
VEGETABLES	177
DESSERTS	199
RECIPE INDEX	214

FOREWORD

by Olivia de Havilland

When my son arrived at the age of young bachelorhood, his sister and I gave him a copy of Françoise Bernard's *Les Recettes Faciles (Easy Recipes)*. Benjamin didn't have the volume to himself for very long; in three weeks Gisèle and I had learned from it six wonderful ways to do chicken and we got each dish right on the first try.

Madame Bernard's *Secrets from My French Kitchen* will have a place right alongside it in our culinary library.

INTRODUCTION

Good cooking is an art. And like all art, expertise grows from the perfection of technique, and the embryo professional will spend years of assiduous practice and hard work in restaurant kitchens under the supervision of stern and experienced chefs. But for those of us who cook for ourselves, for our families, and for our guests, the aim is not to become a world-famous chef, but a Cordon Bleu cook who succeeds in everything – or almost everything – we undertake. And this is where I can help.

The more adventurous you are as a cook, the more likely you are to have appreciated that most recipes reach a critical stage to which you have to pay particular attention. This 'trap' has to be recognized and 'sprung' – otherwise the cream sauce will curdle, the meringues will shrivel, the omelette will glue itself to the pan.

After many years I have learned how to pinpoint and cope with these traps, and I can now reveal my 'secrets', which you will find at the end of most of the recipes included in this book. They are really nothing much more than cunning techniques – techniques which professional chefs may take years to acquire – which you can simply apply at that critical moment, to help you succeed.

The recipes in this book are all tried and tested, and the 'secrets', the notes, the advice on organization and presentation, are the keys to success. The recipes themselves are simple and easy to follow; and they have been specially selected to illustrate the 'secrets of my French kitchen'.

Now you can make my 'secrets' yours – they are culled from many years of cooking experience – and they will lead you to discover cooking secrets of your own.

Françoise Bernard

EDITOR'S NOTE

In translating quantities, you will notice that metric equivalents hardly ever convert exactly to pints, pounds and ounces. We have taken the nearest sensible equivalent to achieve a good result in each case. The quantities are given first in metric, then, after an oblique, in avoirdupois (English). The figure in brackets is the American equivalent.

IMPORTANT: All tablespoons and teaspoons are level, unless otherwise stated, and the flour used is plain – unless differently specified. The cream used is fresh, not processed.

STARTERS (APPETIZERS)

Some of these dishes may be familiar but most of them are typically French. Choose a starter that contrasts with your main course dish – soup or fish before meat, or a terrine or pasta before fish. The recipes range from terrines to vegetables, fish and shellfish and finally, because no French cookbook would be complete without one, an omelette. Some of these recipes make good light lunch or supper dishes too, when accompanied by a vegetable or green salad.

CHEESE & ONION SOUP WITH PORT WINE

Preparation and cooking: 40 minutes   Hot starter

For 4
3 large onions
25g/1oz (*2 Tbsp*) butter or margarine
1 heaped tablespoon flour
½ glass dry white wine
1½ litres/2½ pints (*3 pints*) hot water
1 beef bouillon cube
4 thin slices bread
4 tablespoons port wine
1-2 egg yolks
75g/3oz (¾ *cup*) grated gruyère cheese
Salt and pepper

1. Finely slice the onions. Cook them slowly in butter or margarine until transparent. Shake over the flour and stir with a wooden spoon until the mixture begins to brown slightly.
2. Add the dry white wine, the water, the bouillon cube, and season with a little salt and pepper and leave to boil for about 15 minutes. Meanwhile toast the bread.
3. In an ovenproof soup tureen mix the port and egg yolks. Pour the onion soup into the tureen, stirring continuously. Place the pieces of toast on top and sprinkle over the grated cheese. Brown under the grill (broiler) or at the top of a very hot oven.

Quick Method: Use dried onion rings, which are soaked in water before cooking.

Note: A drop of water on the onions will stop them browning if they start to cook too fast. Make very sure that the soup tureen is ovenproof (usually ovenproof porcelain or earthenware) as it has to withstand very high temperatures.

 The Secret of a good thick, layer of browned cheese on onion soup: The grated gruyère should be sprinkled over the toast on top of the soup, as this will float and prevent the cheese from sinking.

WHITE FISH SOUP

Preparation and cooking: 1¼ hours   Hot starter
In a pressure cooker: 25 minutes

For 4
1¼kg/2lb white fish
  (eg. halibut, cod etc)
2 onions
3–4 tablespoons olive oil
2 tomatoes
3 cloves garlic
Bouquet garni
A sprig of rosemary
1 tablespoon pastis
  (Pernod or Ricard)
A little saffron
2–3 tablespoons vermicelli
  (optional)
Salt and pepper
Grated gruyère cheese
Garlic-flavoured croûtons
  (see method)

1. Gut and clean fish (*see page 138*) but leave the heads on.
2. Put the quartered onions, olive oil, diced tomatoes and garlic into a pan with the bouquet garni and sprig of rosemary. Put in the fish. Cook over a high heat, breaking up the fish with a wooden spoon during cooking.
3. After about 12 minutes, when the fish is completely flaky, add 2 litres (3½ pints) of water, the pastis, salt, pepper and lastly, saffron. Boil up and continue to cook for 30 minutes.
4. Put the soup through a blender to powder the bones. You can thicken it with the vermicelli if you wish. Bring back to the boil, and if using the vermicelli, add it now. Leave to boil for 3 minutes. Serve with croûtons and grated gruyère cheese.

To make croûtons: fry cubes of dry white bread in oil in a frypan (skillet) or deep fryer, until golden. Drain on absorbent kitchen paper, sprinkle with salt and serve with the soup.

Quick Method: Cook in a pressure cooker for 10 minutes. Put through the blender. Saves time and fish. Just before serving, thicken with a little flour mixed with 1–2 tablespoons of thick cream.

The Secret of a good fish soup: Mashing the fish during cooking with a wooden spoon reduces it to a soup consistency. Every bit of flavour is thus extracted, giving an incomparable taste to the soup. To keep it light and soft: keep it on the boil.

INDIVIDUAL BRETON PÂTÉS

Preparation and cooking: 45 minutes   Hot starter

For 4
300g/12 oz minced (ground) veal
2 large onions, finely chopped
20g/¾ oz *(scant Tbsp)* butter or margarine
50g/2 oz *(2 cups)* fresh white breadcrumbs
2 tablespoons milk
Mixed herbs (fresh or dried) – e.g. parsley, tarragon, thyme and sage
100g/4 oz lean bacon, diced
1 egg, beaten
1 tablespoon brandy
Salt and pepper

1. Sauté the onions in the butter or margarine. Soak the bread in the milk.
2. In a bowl, mix the onions with the veal, herbs soaked bread and bacon. Bind with the egg, add the brandy and seasoning.
3. Cut four large squares of kitchen foil, place a portion of the mixture on each and seal, not too tightly, by folding up the corners into parcels. Place in a hot oven (Gas Mark 7, 425°F, 215°C) for about 30 minutes. Serve hot or cold in its 'papillote' of foil, with toast, if liked.

 The Secret of perfect pâtés: Do not fold the foil too tightly, or the pâté may burst out in cooking.

CHICKEN LIVER TERRINE

Preparation and cooking: 1 hour 30 minutes Cold starter
To marinate: 24 hours

For 6 to 8
350g/¾lb chicken livers
125g/4½ oz fresh pork
125g/4½ oz shoulder of veal
100g/4 oz thin slices pork fat
50g/2 oz streaky bacon

The marinade
Thyme
3–4 bay leaves
2 pinches grated nutmeg
1 glass port wine
1 liqueur glass brandy
1 tablespoon oil
Salt and pepper

Rectangular terrine dish

1. The day before put the livers to marinate in the marinade ingredients listed.
2. *Next day.* Keeping 3 or 4 livers on one side, mince (grind) the meat very finely, passing it through several times, if necessary. Mash the minced meat into the marinating liquid, and season generously with salt and pepper. Dice the 3 or 4 remaining livers.
3. Line the terrine dish with the pork fat (a) and then pack in half the minced mixture. Add a layer of diced liver, then the rest of the mince, and top with bay leaves, thyme and the streaky bacon (b). Cover tightly and place in a roasting tin filled with water. Cook in a moderate oven (Gas Mark 4, 350°F, 180°C) for about 1 hour. Remove lid and press pâté in the mould under a 1 kilo (2 lb.) kitchen weight. Leave until cold.

Note: Any poultry liver can be used in making a terrine, but chicken or goose livers are known to be the best.

The Secrets of making a good terrine: A terrine must be well seasoned. Taste it raw to make sure it is to your liking. It will taste better if it includes a whole cooked egg and 2 tablespoons of brandy.
A piece of pork fat placed on top before cooking makes a good surface jelly. But do not leave it on the terrine once cooked; remove it when taken out of the oven. To make sure the terrine is cooked, pierce right through with a thin skewer. It should come out hot right to the tip. When pressing the terrine after cooking, do not use too heavy a weight or the fat will rise to the top leaving a dry centre. Leave for 2 or 3 days before eating.

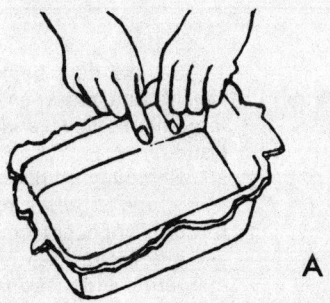

A

B

TURKEY TERRINE

Preparation and cooking: 3 hours   Cold starter
To marinate: 24 hours

For 10 or 12
½ turkey, 2–2½kg/4–5 lb in weight
500g/1lb belly of pork
140g/5oz (*scant ⅔ cup*) margarine
300g/11oz fat bacon
500g/1lb streaky bacon
A piece of pork fat
Salt and pepper

The marinade
¼ litre/½ pint (*1¼ cups*) dry white wine
1 glass of port wine
2 tablespoons oil
1 carrot
1 onion
2 shallots
4 cloves of garlic
2 cloves
Thyme, Bay leaf, Parsley
Pepper

A 23 cm (9 in.) long terrine dish or loaf tin.

1. Several days beforehand bone the raw turkey. Marinate the meat, with the pork, in the listed ingredients. Cover and leave in a cool place for 24 hours.
2. Remove and drain the meat and keep some thin strips of white meat aside. Pass the meat through a mincer (grinder) twice, if necessary, to achieve a firm, smooth mixture. Mash in the margarine and season with salt and pepper.
3. Line the terrine dish with the streaky bacon slices and fill it with the minced (ground) meat, in alternating layers of light and dark meat. Place the piece of pork fat over the top and cover the dish. Put this into a deep ovenproof dish full of water, and cook in a very hot oven (Gas Mark 8–9, 450°–475°F, 230° – 240°C) for 1 hour 30 minutes. Remove the rind after cooking and leave terrine in a cool place for several days before serving.

Note: You may find buying turkey pieces easier than boning out a raw turkey. Buy them to the stated weight, allowing a little less if the pieces are boneless.

The Secret of removing the terrine from the dish in which it has been cooked: Firstly, scrape away the excess fat on the surface. Slide the blade of a knife round the inside of the dish to loosen the terrine, then place the base of the dish in a pan of hot water for 3 to 4 minutes. Up-turn the terrine on to the serving dish. Within a few minutes the contents should come away easily from the dish in one piece.

RABBIT TERRINE

Preparation and cooking: 2¼ hours   Cold starter
To marinate: 12 hours

To 1 saddle of rabbit use:
750g/1¾lb raw pork
100g/4oz streaky bacon
100g/4oz pork fat
Salt and pepper

The marinade
¼ litre/½ pint (1¼ cups) white wine
1 liqueur glass madeira
1 carrot
1 onion
1 clove garlic
1 tablespoon oil
Bouquet garni
Pepper

1. Marinate the rabbit overnight in all the marinade ingredients as listed.
2. Finely chop the pork and season with salt and pepper. Add just enough of the strained marinade liquid to obtain a soft, but not too runny, mixture. Place slices of bacon on the bottom of the terrine dish. Drain the rabbit meat, chop, but do not bone it, and pack the pieces tightly into the terrine dish. Cover with the rest of the chopped meat. Place a large strip of pork fat on the top and cook by placing in a roasting tin half-full of warm water in a moderate oven (Gas Mark 4, 350°F, 180°C) for about 1 hour 30 minutes. Serve cold in the terrine dish.

The Secret of the superb quality of this terrine: The bones, cooked with the terrine, give it a lot of taste and also exude some delicious jelly. This terrine, should not be served in slices, like other terrines or pâtés because of the bones. Serve it with a roasting fork in portions, so that the bones can be identified and removed.

HAM CORNETS

Preparation and cooking: 45 minutes   Hot starter

For 4
4 thin slices cooked ham
100g/4oz. soft liver pâté

The madeira sauce
1 onion, chopped
40g/1½oz, (*3 Tbsp*) butter or margarine
30g/1oz, (*2 Tbsp*) flour
⅓ litre/scant ¾ pint (*scant pint*) white wine or stock
1 glass madeira
Salt and pepper

The fresh pea purée
600g/1lb 4oz fresh or frozen peas
1 lettuce
1 teaspoon sugar
2 tablespoons thick cream
20g/¾ oz (*scant Tbsp*) butter
Salt and pepper

1. *The madeira sauce.* Lightly soften the onion in the butter or margarine. Sprinkle with flour and stir until pale brown. Moisten with the white wine or stock, and season with salt and pepper. Stir until the mixture thickens, then leave to simmer for 15 minutes over a very low heat. Five minutes before the end of the cooking time, add the madeira.
2. Prepare the cornets (see illustrations) and fill with liver pâté, using a forcing bag or a teaspoon. Put them on a dish on top of a pan of boiling water to warm through while you make the purée.
3. *Fresh pea purée.* Boil the peas and lettuce leaves for 10 minutes in a pan of water with the salt and sugar. Drain and put through a vegetable strainer to get rid of the skins. Beat in the cream, pepper and butter.
4. Serve ham cornets with very hot madeira sauce poured over them, and the pea purée separately.

8 cornet or cream horn moulds: forcing bag and 1cm (½in.) plain pipe

☞ *The Secret of madeira sauce which is strongly flavoured:* The wine is added in the last 5 minutes or, if you prefer, half is added halfway through the cooking time and the remainder at the end, so that the flavour does not evaporate in the steam from the sauce.

a. Roll the slice of ham into a cornet shape and push into mould. Any fat should be on the outside of the roll.

b. Fit second mould inside ham.

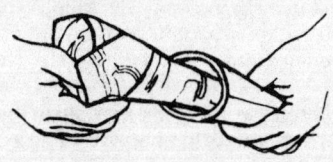

c. Trim all round top. Remove inner mould.

d. Fill with liver pâté using a forcing bag, and then slide cornet out of mould on to the hand so as not to spoil the shape.

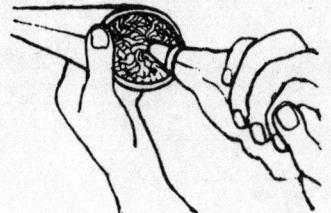

HAM WITH CREAM & PORT WINE

Preparation and cooking: 20 minutes   Hot starter

For 4
4 thick slices of cooked ham
1 large glass port wine
1 can (538g, or 1lb 3oz) spinach or same quantity of frozen spinach
25g/1oz (*2 Tbsp*) butter
1 teaspoon flour
Salt and pepper

The sauce
2 tablespoons thick cream
1 teaspoon flour
Salt and pepper

1. Lay the slices of ham in a baking dish and cover them with port wine. Cover with a piece of kitchen foil. Heat in a slow oven (Gas Mark 4–5, 350°F, 180°C) for about 15 minutes, then put on one side and keep hot, draining off the port to use in the sauce.
2. Meanwhile, melt the butter in a pan, stir in the flour over the heat and add the well drained spinach, salt and pepper. Leave to simmer.
3. *The sauce.* Heat the cream in a small pan with the flour, salt and pepper and the port which was used in heating the ham. Bring to the boil and allow to boil for a few minutes, stirring all the time. Then pour the piping hot sauce on to the ham. Serve with the spinach.

Note: Sherry, madeira, vermouth or a sweet wine can be used instead of port.

 The Secret of sliced ham which does not curl up when re-heated: The wine in which the ham is re-heated should never boil. This is why the dish is covered with foil in case the oven gets too hot.

QUENELLES

Preparation and cooking: 35 minutes   Hot starter
Waiting time: 1 hour

For 4
400g/14oz white fish fillets (fresh haddock or cod)
25g/1oz (*2 Tbsp*) butter or margarine
2 egg whites
2 tablespoons thick cream
Cayenne pepper
Salt and pepper

The sauce
¼ litre/½ pint (¾ *pint*) béchamel sauce (see method) made with:
¼ litre/½ pint (¾ *pint*) milk
1 onion, sliced
1 bayleaf
6 peppercorns
Blade of mace
25g/1oz (*2 Tbsp*) butter
30g/1oz (*2 Tbsp*) flour
Salt and pepper

50g/2oz (½ *cup*) grated gruyère cheese
1 tablespoon thick cream

1. Cut up the raw fish fillets and put through a blender to make a fish purée. Turn into a large bowl.
2. Little by little, add the egg whites (unbeaten) working them in well with a wooden spoon for about 5 minutes. The consistency of the mixture should be that of a very thick mayonnaise. Then add salt, pepper, a pinch or two of cayenne and the cream. Mix well and chill in the refrigerator for at least 1 hour.
3. *The sauce:* Heat the milk in a pan with the onion, bayleaf, peppercorns and mace. Cover pan and leave on very gentle heat for 5 minutes. Strain and set aside. Heat the butter in a clean pan, add the flour and stir until creamy. Add half the flavoured milk, stir until blended with a sauce whisk or wooden spoon and add the rest of the milk. Adjust seasoning and boil for a couple of minutes.
4. *Cooking:* Bring a large saucepan of salted water to the boil and when just boiling, drop in tablespoonfuls of the quenelle mixture, not too many at a time as they need room to expand. Leave to just simmer for 8 to 10 minutes. Drain each thoroughly on absorbent kitchen paper.

5. Arrange the quenelles on an ovenproof gratin dish. Beat the cheese into the sauce and add the cream. Pour over quenelles, dot with butter or margarine and put into a hot oven (Gas Mark 6–7, 400° – 425°F, 200° – 220°C) for 12 minutes before serving.

The quenelles may be not only prepared but cooked in advance as well. Leave in their cooking liquid in the refrigerator and simply put into the oven with the sauce to heat through before serving.

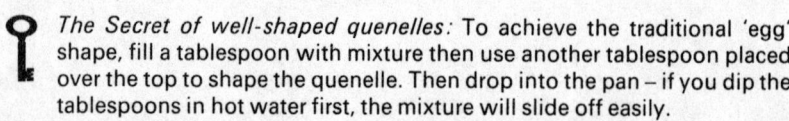 *The Secret of well-shaped quenelles:* To achieve the traditional 'egg' shape, fill a tablespoon with mixture then use another tablespoon placed over the top to shape the quenelle. Then drop into the pan – if you dip the tablespoons in hot water first, the mixture will slide off easily.

FLOATING SCAMPI

Preparation and cooking: 45 minutes   Hot or cold starter

For 4
24 scampi or Dublin Bay prawns
1 carrot
1 onion
25g/1oz (*2 Tbsp*) butter or margarine
1 bottle dry white wine
Bouquet garni
5 peppercorns
A pinch or two cayenne pepper
Salt

1. *The court-bouillon.* Peel and slice the carrot and onion. Cook gently in a large pan with the butter or margarine until the onion is transparent. Add the wine, the same amount of water, the bouquet garni, salt, peppercorns and a pinch of cayenne. Cover and leave to boil gently for 30 minutes.
2. Wash the scampi thoroughly in running water and carefully remove the shells (if fresh).
3. Plunge the scampi into the boiling court-bouillon and leave to cook for 10 minutes. Serve them hot or cold in the reduced court-bouillon (hence 'floating').

Note: If you can find frozen Pacific prawns, these are ideal for this recipe. In this case, reduce the quantity to 3–4 per person, cook for at least 20 minutes in the court-bouillon.

SCAMPI À LA CRÈME

Preparation and cooking: 30 minutes   Hot starter

For 4
1 lb. scampi or Dublin Bay prawns
1-2 tablespoons oil
1 liqueur glass brandy
125g/5-6 fl. oz (generous $\frac{2}{3}$ *cup*) thick cream
Juice of $\frac{1}{2}$ lemon
Cayenne pepper
Salt and pepper

1. Sauté the scampi or prawns, in a little oil, pour over the brandy, bring to the boil and set alight. Add the cream, a little salt and a pinch of cayenne pepper.
2. Place the scampi on a warm serving dish. Boil up the sauce then strain. Add the lemon juice and pour over the scampi. Serve immediately.

Plain boiled rice makes the perfect accompaniment.

Note: If using Dublin Bay prawns, or crayfish – also suitable for this recipe – sauté them before removing the head shells, and putting them, unpeeled, on the serving dish. Provide a finger bowl for each guest.

If using frozen scampi, allow to thaw in the refrigerator for at least 12 hours before cooking.

PRAWN FRITTERS

Preparation and cooking: 20 minutes   Hot starter

For 4
450g/¾ pint (*1 pint*) fresh or peeled prawns

The batter
5 heaped tablespoons flour
1 egg + 2 egg whites
1 tablespoon oil
2.15dl/7½fl. oz (*1 cup*) light beer
¼ teaspoon salt

Deep fat fryer

1. *The batter:* Put the flour, whole egg, oil and salt into a bowl. Mix well with a wooden spoon. Add the beer, little by little, until you have a very thick batter (much thicker than for pancakes). Beat the egg whites until they hold stiff peaks just before using the batter and carefully fold them in.
2. Dip the prawns immediately in the batter and plunge into very hot oil in a deep fat fryer.
3. As soon as they turn ivory-coloured, drain on to absorbent kitchen paper. Serve very hot.

Quick method: Use frozen shellfish and drop into not-too-hot oil so they can defrost and cook at the same time.

Variation: Leave the prawns to marinate in oil, lemon juice, spices, salt and pepper for 1 hour. Cook as above and they will have an even more subtle flavour.

 The Secret of crisp batter: The frying oil must be very hot. Test by dropping a cube of bread into the pan. It should brown in less than 60 seconds. The maximum recommended temperature for oil is 375°F (188°C).

OYSTER COCKTAIL

Preparation: 30 minutes   Cold starter

For 4
24 oysters

The sauce
2 tablespoons tomato ketchup (catsup)
1 tablespoon chilli sauce
1 teaspoon ready-made mayonnaise
1 teaspoon creamed horseradish
Paprika (optional)
Salt and pepper

Crushed ice (3–4 dozen cubes should be sufficient, depending on size of plates)

1. *The sauce*. Whisk up the ingredients for the sauce so that it is fluffy and well blended. It should look like a runny mayonnaise. Pour into 4 small individual bowls or ramekins.
2. Crush the ice by placing it on a clean cloth. Wrap it up and hold it tightly while you smash it with a rolling pin on a hard firm surface. Arrange it on four large individual dishes. Place a bowl of sauce in the centre of each.
3. Open the oysters and arrange 6 around each sauce bowl on top of the ice. Guests lightly dip the oysters into the sauce as they eat.

Note: A squeeze of lemon juice on each oyster will sharpen the taste.

The Secret of crushed ice which lasts: Use ice straight from the freezer at 0°F (–18°C). It will be more fragile and crush easily, and it also melts much less quickly than ice from the refrigerator.

MOULES MARINIÈRE

Preparation and cooking: 45 minutes   Hot starter

For 4
4 litres/7 pints (*9 pints*) mussels
15g/½oz. (*1 Tbsp*) butter
2 shallots, finely chopped
1 glass dry white wine
1 heaped tablespoon chopped parsley
Pepper

1. Clean the mussels well by scrubbing the shells and removing the 'beard' from the side of the shell. Put in a large pan with the butter, chopped shallots and white wine. Put the pan over high heat for a few minutes to open the mussels, stirring them round gently two or three times during cooking.
2. When the mussels are open, remove them from the pan and discard any with the shell still closed. Reserve the cooking juices. Place the mussels in a deep, warm serving dish.
3. Thoroughly strain the cooking juices through a fine strainer and replace over the heat. Allow to boil for a few seconds, add pepper, then pour over the mussels. Sprinkle with chopped parsley and serve.

Note: To help your guests, remove one shell from each mussel before arranging on the serving dish. Provide a finger bowl for each guest.

 The Secret of extra special moules marinière : Add a little fresh cream to the sauce over the heat at the last minute.

MUSSEL QUICHE

Preparation and cooking: 1 hour 15 minutes   Hot starter

For 4
Shortcrust pastry
150g/5oz (*1¼ cups*) flour
75g/3oz (*scant ⅓ cup*) butter or margarine
½ glass water (approx)
½ teaspoon salt

The filling
1½ litres/2½ pints (*2 pints*) mussels (*see page 158*)
½ glass dry white wine
1 onion, chopped
2 eggs
3–4 tablespoons thick cream
1 tablespoon chopped parsley
Pepper
Salt (optional)

20cm (9-in.) diameter flan ring on a baking sheet

1. Prepare the pastry (*see recipe for Scallops in Pastry Shells on page 154*). Line into a buttered flan ring. Prick the base and put into the refrigerator to chill.
2. Scrub the mussels well and open them by bringing them to the boil in the white wine with the onion. Remove from shells, discarding any that have not opened. Put the cooking liquid through a fine sieve lined with kitchen paper to catch any sand, and set aside. Arrange the mussels in the flan.
3. Beat the eggs with the fresh cream, chopped parsley and one glass of the mussel liquid. Pepper but only add salt if necessary after tasting. Pour this over the mussels and cook in a hot oven (Gas Mark 6–7, 400°F–425°F, 200–220°C) for 30–35 minutes.

The Secrets: Fresh thick cream which does not detract from the delicate flavour is added liberally to the beaten eggs; quick cooking; and eating straightaway.

MACARONI RING SALAD

Preparation and cooking: 30 minutes
Standing time: 15 minutes

Cold starter or side salad

For 4
250g/10oz macaroni rings
1–2 tablespoons olive oil
A few pickled gherkins
A few radishes
20 stoned green olives
3 small tomatoes
2 hard-boiled eggs
Mixed herbs, fresh or dried
Salt

The mayonnaise
1 egg yolk
$\frac{1}{4}$ litre/$\frac{1}{2}$ pint ($1\frac{1}{4}$ *cups*) oil
$\frac{1}{4}$ teaspoon salt
1 teaspoon strong mustard
1 teaspoon white wine vinegar, or cold water
1 teaspoon paprika
1 teaspoon tomato ketchup (catsup)
Pepper

1. Cook the pasta in salted boiling water. Drain when cooked and mix in the oil. Put in the refrigerator to cool.
2. Slice the gherkins, radishes and the green olives. Skin and quarter the tomatoes and hard-boiled eggs and chop the mixed herbs (if using fresh).
3. Prepare a strong but fairly thin mayonnaise by combining egg yolk, oil, salt, pepper and mustard (*see page 28*). If need be, add a drop of white wine vinegar or cold water at the end. Then add the paprika and tomato ketchup (catsup). Mix the mayonnaise with the chilled macaroni, gherkins, radishes, mixed herbs and olives. Decorate with the tomatoes and eggs.

Note: The salad can be augmented with diced cooked ham or chicken breast, as well as various shellfish, crabmeat, etc.

The Secret of macaroni ring salad: The oil in which the macaroni is mixed as soon as it is drained, and the consistency of the mayonnaise, helps to bind the salad together.

ARTICHOKES & PINK SAUCE

Preparation and cooking: 40 minutes Cold starter
Allow time to cool

For 4
4 artichokes
Salt

The pink sauce
100g/4oz. roquefort cheese
2–3 tablespoons tomato ketchup (catsup)
A few drops of Tabasco
1 teaspoon brandy
1 tablespoon vinegar or lemon juice
2 tablespoons thick cream

1. *To cook the artichokes.* Wash them well and prune the tops of the leaves with scissors to equal lengths. Tie a piece of strong string tightly round the centre of each artichoke to keep the leaves together while cooking. Cook for 20 to 25 minutes in boiling salted water, drain and cool.
2. *The pink sauce.* Grate the cheese finely and mix it with all the other sauce ingredients.
3. Remove the choke and the outer leaves so as to leave the heart and a crown of thick leaves. Pour sauce into the middle of each and serve.

Note: This sauce can be used with many other cold starters such as hard-boiled eggs, prawns, celery, asparagus, etc. If you find roquefort cheese difficult to obtain, you can use Danish Blue instead.

 The Secret of artichoke leaves which stay firmly closed after cooking: To ensure that the leaves do not spread and bend outwards in cooking bind them tightly with string like a bush in winter. Cut the string and remove before serving.

ASPARAGUS MILANAISE

Preparation and cooking: 40 minutes   Hot starter

For 4
1kg/2lb fresh asparagus
30g/1½oz (*3 Tbsp*) butter
50g/2oz (½ *cup*) parmesan cheese, grated
Salt and pepper

1. Peel the asparagus with a fine vegetable peeler. Wash and cook for 12–15 minutes in boiling salted water to cover. To do this, tie the asparagus into a bundle with fine string round the top and base. Put butter to melt over low heat.
2. Drain asparagus well, remove string, and place, side by side, while still very hot, on an ovenproof gratin dish. Sprinkle with parmesan from the green tip to halfway along. Pour over the melted butter and place in a hot oven (Gas Mark 6–7, 400–425°F, 212°C) for a few minutes to brown the cheese.

Note: For speed, use the same quantity of canned asparagus. It should not need boiling.

The Secret of asparagus tender enough to cut: Fresh asparagus should be carefully peeled and not just scraped, from just below the tip to the base. Then break it near the base (asparagus will break off at the point where it gets tough).

STUFFED AUBERGINES

Preparation and cooking: Hot starter

For 4
4 smallish, rounded aubergines
60g/2½oz (*generous ¼ cup*) butter or margarine
200g/8oz ham, raw or cooked
250g/10oz sweet peppers, de-seeded and finely chopped
500g/1lb tomatoes, skinned and finely chopped
1 clove garlic, crushed
Salt and pepper

Deep fat fryer

1. Carefully wipe the aubergines. Cut off the end. Cut them in half lengthways, then with a sharp pointed knife, deeply cut all round the flesh ½ cm (¼ in) from the sides, without piercing the skin (a). Make cuts across the top diagonally at 1 cm (½ in) intervals, then cut again so you have a criss-cross pattern (b). Quickly deep-fry the half aubergines in a deep fat bath for 2 minutes, to part-cook the flesh. Drain them.
2. Remove the flesh in cubes with a small spoon, without piercing the skin, and chop finely.
3. Dice the ham and cook it in a flameproof casserole in half the butter with the peppers, tomatoes and garlic, on a moderate heat for 10 minutes. Add the finely chopped aubergine flesh, season, and cook for a further 5 minutes. Fill the aubergine skins with this stuffing and put them on a buttered ovenproof dish. Place a few dots of butter on each and cook in a hot oven (Gas Mark 6–7, 400°–425°F, 200°–220°C) for 20 minutes.

 The Secret: Is to pile the skins full of the savoury stuffing. The aubergine flesh, when cooked, may turn black, but the ham, bright peppers and tomatoes offset this.

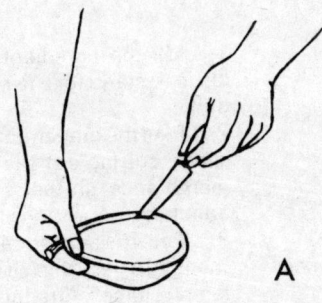

A

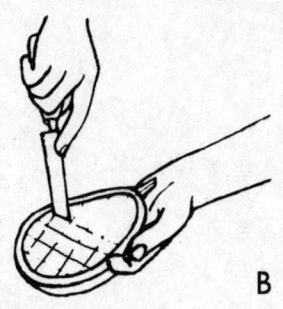

B

AVOCADO AND GRAPEFRUIT SALAD

Preparation and cooking: 20 minutes — Cold starter or side salad

For 4
2 avocado pears
1 grapefruit
1 tomato
½ lemon
1 lettuce heart

The lemon dressing
1 tablespoon lemon juice
2–3 tablespoons oil
1 clove garlic, crushed
Salt and pepper

1. Mix the ingredients for the salad dressing and leave to stand for a few minutes with the crushed garlic.
2. Peel the grapefruit and slice the flesh into thin slices, cutting out each slice between the white membranes, so they slide out without any pith attached.
3. Peel the avocadoes and skin the tomato. Cut them into very thin slices and squeeze over with lemon juice. Arrange the slices of avocado, tomato and grapefruit alternately on a bed of lettuce leaves and season. Just before serving, pour over a little of the dressing. Serve the rest of the dressing separately after straining off the garlic.

The Secret of a crisp salad: Once it has been seasoned, leave in the refrigerator until it is time to eat it. Do not add the dressing until just before serving.

STUFFED AVOCADOES I

Preparation and cooking: 20 minutes   Cold starter

For 4
2 avocado pears
2 large tomatoes
1 onion, chopped
1 teaspoon capers
1 tablespoon white sharp cheese (White Cheshire or Caerphilly)
Juice of 1 lemon
2–3 tablespoons oil
Salt and pepper

1. Halve the avocadoes. Remove the flesh carefully without bruising the skin and rub the insides with lemon juice to stop them turning black. Put the skins in the refrigerator.
2. Skin the tomatoes and remove the seeds. Dice the flesh of the tomatoes and avocadoes, and mix well with the chopped onion, capers, cheese, lemon juice, salt, pepper and oil. Leave to stand in a cool place.
3. To serve, fill the avocado skins with the mixture.

The Secret of an avocado which does not turn black: Cut it with a stainless steel knife which, ideally, should be well sprinkled with lemon juice.

STUFFED AVOCADOES II

Preparation and cooking: 45 minutes
Standing time: 1 hour

Cold starter

For 4
- 2 avocado pears
- 2·8dl/½ pint (*1 cup*) frozen prawns

The stock
- ½ litre/¾ pint (*1 pint*) water
- 1 onion, peeled
- 1 carrot, peeled
- 1 clove
- 1 teaspoon vinegar
- Bouquet garni
- 4 peppercorns
- Salt

- 1·4dl/¼ pint (¾ *cup*) mayonnaise
- A few drops Tabasco, or a pinch of cayenne pepper
- Mixed herbs (fresh or dried)
- 1 lemon
- ½ cap canned pimiento
- 1 tablespoon capers
- 4 lettuce leaves
- Salt and pepper

1. *To cook the frozen prawns.* Put the frozen prawns and all the stock ingredients in the measured water. Bring very slowly to the boil, then leave to simmer very gently for 5–7 minutes. Allow to cool completely in the stock.
2. Make the mayonnaise (*see page 21*), or use ready-made mayonnaise, and add Tabasco or cayenne pepper, mixed herbs, juice of half the lemon, the pimiento, finely sliced, a few capers and the drained and chopped prawns.
3. Slice the avocado pears in two lengthways just before serving and remove stones. Line each half with a lettuce leaf and pile the prawn salad mixture on top. Cut off 4 thin slices of lemon. Make a cut in each lemon slice from the peel to the centre and twist it to place one on top of each stuffed avocado.

Organization: The filling can be prepared several hours in advance, or even the day before, as long as it is kept in a refrigerator. Only section 3 above has to be done at the last moment.

The Secret of deep frozen prawns that do not lose their taste: They must be cooked very slowly in the stock with a lot of flavouring, then left in the stock to cool. They can be left in the stock overnight, if kept in the refrigerator.

GRAPEFRUIT WITH CRAB

Preparation and cooking: 30–45 minutes   Cold starter

For 4
1 can (213g/7½oz) crabmeat
2 large grapefruit
50g/2oz (⅓ *cup*) cooked rice
16 stoned black or green olives
Salt and pepper

The mayonnaise
1 egg yolk
¼ litre/½ pint (1¼ *cups*) oil
1 teaspoon strong mustard
1 teaspoon white wine vinegar, or cold water
A pinch of cayenne pepper (optional)
Salt and pepper

1. Cook the rice for 15–18 minutes in plenty of boiling, salted water. As soon as it is cooked, rinse under cold water to cool it, then drain.
2. *The mayonnaise.* Whisk together the egg yolk, salt, pepper and mustard until a smooth, bland consistency is reached. Add the oil, drop by drop, until the sauce begins to thicken, then add the rest of the oil a little more quickly (in a steady trickle, if using a blender). Stir smoothly the whole time, and add the vinegar or cold water at the end to keep it from separating.
3. Cut each grapefruit in two, cut the flesh away from the sides, using a grapefruit knife, and cut into segments between the white membranes. Remove and discard all the membranes from inside the grapefruit. Chop olives, reserving 4 for decoration.
4. In a bowl, mix the crabmeat, grapefruit segments, rice, chopped olives and mayonnaise. To serve, fill the grapefruit halves with the salad and decorate each with a whole olive.

Note: The ingredients can be prepared in advance if they are kept separately in the refrigerator. Combine them at the last moment and fill the skins. Ready-bought mayonnaise can be used.

The Secret of a successful salad: Drain the crabmeat well before mixing, and use just enough mayonnaise to coat. Do not mix too long before serving. A sprinkling of chopped parsley is an optional extra.

STUFFED TOMATOES

Preparation and cooking: 1 hour   Hot starter

For 4
4 large or 8 smaller tomatoes
25g/1oz (*2 Tbsp*) butter or margarine
½ glass milk
50g/2oz (*2–3 slices*) stale bread
150–200g/5oz (*1–1½ cups*) minced (ground) cooked meat or sausagemeat
1 egg
2 tablespoons chopped parsley
1 onion, chopped
1 clove garlic
50g/2oz (*2 cups*) breadcrumbs
Salt and pepper

1. Cut off the tops of the tomatoes at the opposite end to the stalk. Hollow out with a teaspoon, sprinkle inside lightly with a little salt and turn upside-down to drain. Warm the milk and soak the bread in it.
2. In a bowl, put the meat, the egg, chopped parsley, chopped onion and garlic. Season with salt and pepper. Add the soaked bread and mix well together. Pack into the tomatoes.
3. Lightly butter an ovenproof gratin dish and place the tomatoes on it. Sprinkle with breadcrumbs and dot with butter or margarine. Cook in a moderate oven (Gas Mark 5, 375°F, 190°C) for 30 minutes. Replace the tops on the tomatoes and cook for a further 10 minutes.

Note: If the filling is too stiff, moisten with the juice from the tomatoes. (French tomatoes are much larger than ours, so allow two per person.)

The Secret of tomatoes that do not burst in the oven: Cut off the top opposite the stalk – this makes them stand firm. Once filled, they should be placed, close together, in the dish in the oven, so they have no room to tilt over.

SAVOURY TOMATO QUICHE

Preparation and cooking: 1 hour Hot starter

The pastry
150g/6oz (*1½ cups*) flour
100g/4oz. (*½ cup*) butter or margarine
A little water
½ teaspoon salt

The filling
500g/1lb tomatoes, skinned
1 large onion, finely chopped
1 clove garlic
Bouquet garni
Salt and pepper

The mornay sauce
20g/¾oz. (*¾ Tbsp*) butter or margarine
1 scant tablespoon flour
¼ litre/½ pint (*¾ pint*) milk
50g/2oz grated gruyère cheese
Salt and pepper

17 cm (7 in) diameter flan ring on a baking sheet

1. *The pastry.* Rub together the flour, salt and fat with the fingertips until the mixture looks like fine breadcrumbs. Add enough water just to mix. Knead for a few minutes.
2. Roll out the pastry and line the flan ring. Place a round of kitchen foil over the base and bake for 20 to 30 minutes in a hot oven (Gas Mark 6–7, 400° – 425°F, 200° – 220°C).
3. *The filling.* Simmer the peeled tomatoes, chopped onion, crushed garlic, bouquet garni, salt and pepper in a pan over low heat for 45 minutes.
4. *The mornay sauce.* Melt the butter over a low heat in a pan. Remove from the heat and stir in the flour until you have a smooth paste. Add a little milk and blend in with the paste. Add the rest of the milk and stir until boiling. Remove from the heat and add the grated gruyère.
5. Fill the tart with the tomato mixture; pour over the sauce and return to a hot oven (Gas Mark 6–7, 400° – 425°F, 200° – 220°C) for a few minutes to brown.

Note: The foil over the base of the pastry case should prevent it rising during cooking.

The Secret of thickening a runny tomato filling: Boil it up quickly without covering, and it will thicken and reduce.

EGGS EN COCOTTE ROQUEFORT

Preparation and cooking: 25 minutes   Hot or cold starter

For 4
4 eggs
100g/4oz (½ *cup*) roquefort or Danish Blue cheese, crumbled
2 tablespoons thick cream
25g/1oz (*2 Tbsp*) butter or margarine
Salt and pepper

4 individual ramekins

1. Beat the eggs with the cream, salt and pepper and finely crumbled cheese.
2. Well butter the 4 ramekins, divide the egg mixture between them and cook in a roasting tin half-full of warm water (bain-marie) in a hot oven (Gas Mark 6–7, 400° – 425°F, 210° – 220°C) for 20 minutes.

The cocottes will un-mould easily when they come out of the oven. Serve warm, just as they are, or with a tomato sauce (*see page 167*).

Variation: Serve them cold, unmoulded on to lettuce leaves, or a green salad, and decorate each with a halved walnut.

The Secret of un-moulding the eggs easily: Plenty of butter in the ramekins should help. Otherwise, slip a knife dipped in hot water around the edge of each.

PORTUGUESE EGG TIMBALE

Preparation and cooking: 1 hour   Hot starter or supper dish

For 4–6
6 eggs
¾ litre/1¼ pints (*1½–1¾ pints*) milk
Pinch of grated nutmeg
½ teaspoon salt
25g/1oz (*2 Tbsp*) butter
Pepper

The tomato sauce
500g/1lb fresh tomatoes
1 green pepper
30g/1½oz (*3 Tbsp*) butter or margarine
2 cloves garlic
1 onion
1 tablespoon tomato paste
1 small strong pimiento
Bouquet garni
Salt and pepper

2-pint (1 quart) soufflé dish

1. Set the oven at Gas Mark 7, 425° – 450°F, 220°C. Boil up the milk. Beat the eggs in a bowl (as though you were making an omelette) with the salt, pepper and grated nutmeg. Add the boiled milk little by little. Pass the mixture through a fine strainer.
2. Pour into a buttered soufflé dish. Half-fill a roasting tin with water, and place the soufflé dish in it. Put into pre-set oven and cook for 20–25 mins.
3. *The tomato sauce*. Scald, skin and quarter the tomatoes. Squeeze out juice. Remove the seeds from the green pepper and slice it into thin strips. Heat the butter or margarine in a pan. Chop the garlic and onion and put them in the pan with the tomatoes, pepper, tomato paste, pimiento, bouquet garni, salt and pepper. Turn the heat up high and cook for 20 to 30 minutes, without covering. Put through the blender, or a fine strainer, when cooked, to make a purée.
4. Leave the egg timbale to cool before turning out into a deep dish. Pour over a little of the sauce and serve the remainder, very hot, in a sauceboat.
    Quick method: Add a little peeled and finely chopped tomato flesh and some lemon juice, salt and pepper and dried herbs to a can of Italian tomatoes. Cook for 5 minutes, adding a little arrowroot, soaked in 1 tablespoon cold water.

The Secret of a good egg timbale: It should cook through thoroughly without boiling. That is why, although the oven is hot, it is placed in a roasting tin half-full of water (a bain-marie). This keeps the temperature even. Be careful not to overcook the dish.

THREE FILLINGS FOR HARD-BOILED EGGS

Preparation of each: 15 minutes   Cold starter or supper dish

MUSTARD FILLING
6 hard-boiled eggs
1 tablespoon strong ready-made mustard
2–3 gherkins
50g/2oz ($\frac{1}{4}$ cup) butter
Juice of 1 lemon
Lettuce leaves
Salt and pepper

Peel and slice the eggs in half, lengthwise. Remove the yolks and crush them. Mix the crushed egg yolks with the mustard, finely chopped gherkins, softened butter, salt, pepper and lemon juice. Fill the empty white halves generously with this mixture, heaping it up. Serve on lettuce leaves.

CHIVE FILLING
6 hard-boiled eggs, halved
50g/2oz ($\frac{1}{4}$ cup) softened butter
2 tablespoons chopped chives
Cayenne pepper
12 radishes
Lettuce leaves
Salt and pepper

Mix the softened butter, chives, salt, pepper and a pinch of cayenne with the crushed egg yolks. Fill the halves of egg white with this mixture. Place a radish on top of each. Arrange on a bed of lettuce.

Further decorative ideas:
(a) A couple of shrimps on top of the filling.
(b) A flowerpot of tomato skin and tomato skin flowers with parsley leaves.

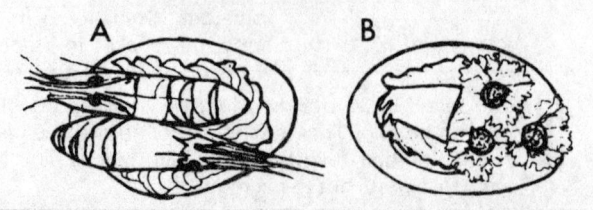

(c) A black olive between two thin triangles of lemon.
(d) A lattice of anchovy and capers on top of the filling.

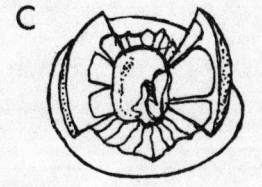

NIÇOISE FILLING

6 hard-boiled eggs, halved
10 stoned black or green olives, chopped
1–2 tablespoons chopped parsley
1 tablespoon anchovy paste
50g/2oz ($\frac{1}{4}$ cup) butter
1 tablespoon strong mustard
24 anchovy fillets
Lettuce leaves
Tomatoes
Mixed green salad
Salt and pepper

Mix the olives and parsley with the crushed egg yolks, anchovy paste, butter, mustard, salt and pepper. Fill the white halves with this mixture generously, piling it up. Garnish with a couple of anchovy fillets in the form of a cross. Arrange on lettuce leaves and serve with tomatoes, skinned, de-seeded and quartered, and mixed green salad.

Party shapes for hard-boiled eggs
1. Cut a thin slice across the base of the white at the 'narrow' end so it sits flat.
2. With a round-ended knife cut just to the yolk (which will resist). Cut all round the yolk in a zig-zag shape.
3. Pull the two halves of white apart. The yolk will remain whole in one of them. Fill the other.

The Secret of perfect hard-boiled eggs: They should cook for exactly 10 minutes, as overcooked boiled eggs acquire a grey film round the yolk. The same thing happens if they are cooked too far in advance. This grey film is edible but hardly attractive.

The Secret of easy peeling: Crack the shells immediately on taking out of the hot water and plunge into cold water. The water seeps underneath the shell which then comes away easily.

OMELETTE

Preparation and cooking: 10 minutes   Hot starter or main course

For 4
8–10 eggs
40g/1½oz (*3 Tbsp*) butter or margarine or 2 tablespoons oil
Salt and pepper

1. Lightly heat the butter or oil in a thick omelette pan. Beat the eggs and pour the melted butter into them. Season and beat well in.
2. Return the pan to the cooker over a high heat. When it is really hot, pour in the egg mixture. Allow to cook, constantly shaking the pan and stirring the mixture with a fork. When the omelette is beginning to dry out round the edges but is still soft in the middle, fold over and turn out on to a dish to serve.

Eight ideas for quick omelette fillers:

Crumbled potato crisps added to the beaten egg mixture before cooking.

Chopped mixed herbs added to the beaten egg.

Canned artichoke hearts, diced and sautéed separately before adding.

Coarsely grated gruyère cheese added before cooking.

Strips of cooked ham and chopped herbs, added to the beaten egg mixture.

Strips of bacon, fried, added to beaten egg.

Canned asparagus tips, drained, heated separately and added, with chopped herbs, halfway through cooking.

Tomatoes, skinned and sliced, sautéed separately then added to the nearly-cooked omelette.

The Secret of non-stick omelettes: Add the melted fat to the egg mixture. Cook in an omelette pan kept solely for the purpose and never wash it (just wipe it out carefully with cooking paper and salt after use), or cook in a non-stick pan.

MAIN COURSE DISHES: MEAT

In this chapter, you will find recipes for beef, pork, veal, lamb and offal (variety meats). Remember that the French often like their roast joints cooked rather rarer than we do, so adjust the cooking time a little if you wish. The cooking times and temperatures may vary according to your particular oven control as every oven is slightly different. One traditional way of tenderizing and flavouring meat before cooking is to marinate it in wine, oil, herbs and seasoning, so we have included two extra marinades at the end of the lamb recipes.

CHOOSING BEEF

Top quality beef can be recognized by:
- its purplish-red flesh (if bright red, it's too fresh and should be kept a few days in the refrigerator before cooking).
- its creamy-coloured fat.
- in lean cuts, by a light marbling of fat through the meat which helps to keep it tender.

ROAST BEEF

FRENCH ROAST BEEF

Cooking time: allow 25–30 minutes per kilo, 12–15 minutes per pound

Pre-set the oven 15 to 25 minutes before putting in the meat. The oven needs to be very hot (Gas Mark 7–8, 425°–450°F, 220°–230°C). Place the joint of beef in a roasting tin just large enough to hold it. If the joint is lean, cook it in a little butter or margarine. Turn and baste the meat while roasting and season with salt and pepper towards the end of cooking time.

The Secrets of tender oven-roast beef: If cooked in too large a tin, the meat spatters its juices all over the oven.

The roast will be more tender if grilled (broiled) slightly first in its roasting tin. This allows the beef to cook in more of its own juices, which will soften the meat.

If wrapped in kitchen foil, the joint can be kept hot for up to half-an-hour after being removed from the oven.

Allow the meat to stand in the turned-off oven for a few minutes. This allows the fibres to relax and makes the meat more tender and easier to carve (you can allow five minutes less cooking time for this).

To improve the flavour, put a sliced onion and a carrot in the baking tin with a little hot water before putting in the meat. Halfway through cooking, add a little more water, pouring it in at the side, not over the meat. When basted with this, the meat's full flavour will develop.

SPIT ROAST BEEF

Cooking: allow slightly longer than in the oven

Pre-heat the rôtisserie (or grill [broiler] if this is being used). The joint should be of equal thickness along its length and evenly balanced on the spit. Sprinkle with a little salt and pepper and start the spit turning. Keep a dish under the meat to catch the juices and use for basting during the first half of cooking.

> *The Secrets of good spit roasting*: If the spit is built into the oven, the door must be left ajar throughout the cooking time.
> To flavour the meat juices, sprinkle the dish under the meat with a few mixed herbs (thyme, bay leaves, rosemary, etc).
> As with an oven roast, a spit roast should be left to 'relax' for a few moments before carving.

POT ROAST OF BEEF

Cooking: allow 25–30 minutes per kilo; 12–15 minutes per pound

Quickly brown the meat all over in a flameproof casserole on high heat, with a little butter or margarine, to seal it.

Then, on a medium-to-high heat, continue cooking without covering. While cooking, turn the meat several times without piercing it. For the last 15 minutes season with salt and pepper, half-cover casserole and lower the heat.

Place the roast on a warmed serving dish. Dilute the cooking juices in the bottom of the casserole with one or two tablespoons of water. Allow to boil for a few moments, adjust seasoning and serve in a sauceboat.

> *The Secrets of casserole roasting*: You can quickly brown the roast first in a pan (skillet) and then continue cooking in the casserole as above. The meat will be crisper on the outside, and you will not run the risk of burning yourself.
> If the piece of meat has a lot of fat around it, drain this off after browning. A little butter or margarine may be added at the end of cooking when the heat is lowered. Add half a diced carrot and 1 or 2 onions, cut into rings, when the meat is starting to roast; a little later, if liked, add a clove or garlic and a bouquet garni.

POT ROAST MEAT

Preparation and cooking: 3 hours 30 minutes
In a pressure cooker: 1 hour 30 minutes

For 1½kg/3lb meat use:
4 leeks
4 carrots
2 turnips
1 small stick of celery
1 onion, stuck with three cloves
1 clove garlic
Bouquet garni
1 marrow bone
Salt

A few pickled gherkins
Rock salt

1. Peel the root vegetables and put them with the celery in a large stewpan with 3 litres /5 pints (*6 pints*) of cold water, the onion, peeled garlic, bouquet garni and salt to taste. As soon as the water starts bubbling, add the joint of meat. Simmer for 2½ to 3 hours (in a pressure cooker: 1½ hours). Skim fat from the surface from time to time.
2. One hour before the end of cooking time, add the marrow bone. Serve the meat, drained, with the vegetables on a hot dish. Serve rock salt, pickled gherkins and the marrow bone jelly separately.

The Secrets of pot roasting: Always use two or three different cuts of meat, so as to mix fat, lean and juicy. Many people like to add a piece of oxtail, as it gives extra flavour and juiciness. Do not forget that boiled meat loses about 40 per cent of its weight in cooking, so too many vegetables and too little meat can spoil the dish. Never leave the vegetables in the stock if you are keeping them; even when left in the refrigerator, the vegetables will quickly give the stock a sour flavour. It should be strained off and kept separately.
For a really good stock, put in the meat when the water is still cold. However, when the meat is put into boiling water, it does taste better, although the stock may not be so good.

GRILLED (BROILED) STEAK

Preparation and cooking: Pre-heat the grill (broiler) a good 10 minutes.

For 4
1 steak per person

Brush the steaks with cooking oil and sprinkle with dried herbs to taste. Place the steaks on the rack fairly close to the heat source and cook for 1 to 2 minutes on each side. Do not add salt or pepper until serving.

The Secret of grilled steak: The thinner the steak, the faster it should be cooked, and the closer the grill (broiler) pan should be to the heat.
   Allow:
1 minute each side; very high heat for steak 1 cm ($\frac{1}{2}$ in) thick.
2–3 minutes each side; high heat for steak 2 cm (1 in) thick.
3–4 minutes each side; medium heat for steak 3 cm ($1\frac{1}{2}$ in) thick.

Grilled (broiled) meat is better if marinated before cooking in a mixture of dried and fresh herbs (thyme, bayleaf, rosemary, parsley, etc), 1 or 2 tablespoons of oil, and a little pepper. Turn the steak several times without piercing, and allow to marinate for at least an hour.

THREE WINE SAUCES FOR STEAK

Preparation and cooking: 10 minutes

The steaks should be cooked first in the pan, then kept hot while the sauce is quickly prepared in the same pan. If grilling (broiling) the steaks, transfer any juices to the frypan or skillet.

SAUCE BERCY

1 chopped shallot, or small onion
¾ glass dry white wine
½ tablespoon tomato paste
1 heaped teaspoon flour
15g/½oz (*1 Tbsp*) butter or margarine
Parsley
Salt and pepper

Cook the chopped shallot in the pan juices over low heat. Add the wine, tomato paste and salt and pepper. Allow to boil for 2 minutes. Mix the butter or margarine into the flour and add to the pan until it starts to thicken, then pour over the steak. Sprinkle with parsley before serving.

SAUCE MARCHAND DE VIN

Use the same ingredients for Sauce Bercy, but use red wine instead of white.

SAUCE LYONNAISE

2–3 onions
40g/1½oz (*3 Tbsp*) butter or margarine
½ glass dry white wine
Salt and pepper

Cut onions in rings and brown in the butter or margarine, in a small pan or skillet. Cook the steaks in a separate pan, remove them and keep hot. Leaving this pan over the heat, pour the wine into the cooking juices and add the cooked onions. Leave to boil for 2 minutes, and pour over the steak before serving.

The Secret of tasty meat sauces which have to be cooked speedily: Add a little rich meat stock from the refrigerator.

PEPPERED STEAK

Preparation and cooking: 50 minutes

For 4
Four 200g/7–8oz fillet steaks
25g/1oz *(2 Tbsp)* butter or margarine
3 tablespoons brandy
Salt
1 tablespoon peppercorns

The sauce
1 veal bone
30g/1½oz *(3 Tbsp)* margarine or cooking oil
1 carrot
1 onion
15g/½oz *(1 Tbsp)* flour
1 glass dry white wine
½ teaspoon tomato paste
Bouquet garni
Salt and pepper

1. *Make the sauce.* Chop the veal bone in two and put into a saucepan over high heat, with the peeled and sliced carrot, onion and margarine or oil. After a few minutes, add the flour and stir until mixture begins to thicken. Add the white wine, a wine glass of water, the tomato paste, bouquet garni and salt and pepper. Stir until boiling. Turn down the heat and allow to simmer gently, uncovered for about 30 minutes. Strain before using.
2. Meanwhile, crush the peppercorns with a rolling pin on a hard work surface. Roll the meat in them so that the crushed peppercorns stick well all over the surface.
3. Cook the steaks to taste in a frypan or skillet over high heat in the butter or margarine. Remove from pan and keep hot.
4. Pour away the juices from the pan, add the brandy and bring to boiling point. Set alight. Then add the strained sauce and re-boil. Pour a little of the sauce over each steak and serve the rest in a sauceboat. Serve with chipped potatoes or French fries.

The Secret of keeping steaks still peppered after cooking: Put the steaks into a *very* hot pan which cooks the outside straightaway.

ENTRECOTE STEAK BORDELAISE

Preparation and cooking: 30 minutes

For 4
2 entrecôte (sirloin) steaks, each about 400g (about 1lb)
25g/1oz (*2 Tbsp*) butter or margarine
50g/2oz (*4 Tbsp*) beef bone marrow
Chopped parsley
Salt and pepper

The sauce Bordelaise
2 shallots, or small onions
50g/2oz (*4 Tbsp*) butter
1 glass red wine
Thyme and bay leaf
1 level teaspoon tomato paste
1 teaspoon flour
Salt and pepper

1. *The sauce.* Finely chop the shallots or onions and fry gently in half the butter. Do not let them brown. Add a quarter of the glass of wine, a pinch of thyme and a bay leaf. Cook over low heat until the liquid is completely reduced. Then add the rest of the wine, the tomato paste, half a glass of water and salt and pepper. Mix the flour with the rest of the butter. Add this, a little at a time, to the sauce to thicken it and leave to simmer over very low heat for 15 minutes.
2. Cut the bone marrow into thick rounds with a knife which has been dipped in boiling water. Place the rounds in a metal sieve and immerse in boiling salted water. Allow to boil for 1 minute. Take off the heat, but wait 2 minutes before draining. Keep hot.
3. Heat the butter or margarine in a large pan. When very hot, but not burning, add the steaks. Leave to cook for about 2 minutes on each side. Season.
4. Remove the steaks and place them on a hot plate with the marrow rounds on top. Pour the sauce into the pan and bring to the boil for a few moments, while stirring in the meat juices with a wooden spoon. Finally, pour the sauce over the steaks and sprinkle with chopped parsley just before serving.

The Secret of shallots which keep their flavour in cooking: They must cook very gently without browning, as browned shallots become bitter and spoil the flavour of the sauce.

BEEF BOURGUIGNON

Preparation and cooking: 2 hours 20 minutes
In a pressure cooker: 50 minutes
Marinate overnight

For 4
1½kg/3lb best stewing (chuck) beef
2 tablespoons oil
30g/1½oz (*3 Tbsp*) butter or margarine
1 heaped tablespoon flour
1 tablespoon tomato paste
2 cloves of garlic
Bouquet garni
1 glass water
Salt and pepper
1kg/2lb potatoes
Chopped parsley

The marinade
1 bottle rough red wine
1 tablespoon oil
1 small carrot
1 onion
2 shallots
1 small stick celery
1 clove garlic
Parsley, thyme and bay leaf
5 black peppercorns
1 clove

1. Put all the marinade ingredients in a large bowl the day before cooking. Cut the meat into cubes and put into the marinade.
2. *Cooking*: Drain the meat, reserving the liquid, and dry with absorbent kitchen paper before browning over a high heat in a little oil. Add the vegetables from the marinade (carrot, onion, shallots, celery) plus the butter or margarine. Leave to cook, uncovered, for 15 minutes. Then sprinkle the flour over and stir gently over a high heat until brown.
3. Pour the liquid from the marinade over the meat and bring to the boil. Add salt, pepper, a glass of water, tomato paste, garlic and bouquet garni. Cover and cook very gently for 2 hours (in a pressure cooker: 50 minutes).
4. Put the potatoes on to boil half an hour before the stew will be ready. Serve the meat and sauce in a deep dish. Hand the potatoes, sprinkled with parsley, separately.

Variations: Towards the end of cooking time, add several other vegetables: onions boiled for 2 minutes, strained, and lightly browned; mushrooms sautéed in butter for 5 minutes; or 1 liqueur glass of brandy to the sauce.

The Secret of a perfect Bourguignon sauce: It should be neither too thin nor too greasy. If the sauce is too thin when cooking is finished, boil it up quickly to reduce and thicken it after removing the meat. If it is too greasy, skim the fat from the surface and re-boil.

FONDUE BOURGUIGNONNE

The great success of this dish lies in the speed of preparation: cube the meat, open a few cans and bottles of spicy sauces and your guests do the rest.
You need a fondue set with a long-handled fork for each guest to dip the cubes of meat in the oil, and an ordinary fork for eating it with pickles.

For 4
900g/2lb fillet of beef
$\frac{1}{2}$ litre/1 pint (*1$\frac{1}{4}$ pints*) oil
Thyme
Bay leaf

A selection of strong sauces and pickles – eg English mustard, capers, gherkins, pickled onions, sweet and mustard pickles, chutney, horseradish cream, tomato sauce, etc. A selection of bland sauces: eg fresh cream with herbs and lemon juice or yoghurt with garlic and chopped chives.

1. Cut the raw meat into smallish cubes. Arrange on 4 large plates. Put the sauces into sauce bowls.
2. Fill the fondue pot two-thirds full of hot oil, and place over its lighted table heater, in the centre of the table. Your guests put a little of their chosen sauces on their plates – spear the raw meat with the long-handled fondue fork and dip it into the hot oil, to cook rapidly. They then transfer it to the other fork to dip in the sauces and eat.

Organization: Two forks each are essential to avoid burning yourself; one for cooking the meat, which gets very hot, and the other for removing the cooked meat and conveying it into the mouth! A side dish of vegetables, or one large mixed salad, will be the only accompaniment needed.

SAUCES FOR FONDUE BOURGUIGNONNE

SAUCE ENRAGÉE
6 hard-boiled eggs
6 hot dried pimientos
6 tablespoons oil
3 tablespoons vinegar
A pinch of saffron
Salt and pepper

Halve the hard-boiled eggs. Remove yolks and crush them in a salad bowl. Finely crush pimientos and gradually beat them into the yolks with the oil, vinegar, saffron, salt and pepper. Lightly heat the resultant purée, stirring continuously. (Use the egg whites in a salad).

SAUCE ROUILLÉ
1 slice of white bread
$\frac{1}{2}$ cup ($\frac{1}{3}$ *cup*) milk
2 cloves of garlic
1 small strong pimiento
6 tablespoons oil
Salt and pepper

Trim the crusts from the bread and soak it in the warm milk. Drain and squeeze out liquid, so you have a thick ball of dough. Crush the garlic with the pimiento and mix into the bread, and season. Little by little, add the oil, beating vigorously with a wooden spoon or electric beater. The final consistency should be like mayonnaise.

FILLET OF BEEF PORTUGAISE

Preparation and cooking: 45 minutes
Marinate for several hours beforehand

For 4
1kg/2lb fillet of beef
250g/8oz button onions or shallots
60g/2½oz *(5 Tbsp)* butter or margarine
150g/6oz *(1 cup)* raisins
A little flour
½ a beef stock cube
Salt and pepper

The marinade
¼ bottle (1¼ cups) port wine
1 shallot, peeled and sliced
1 clove garlic
1 small stick cinnamon
2 pinches of nutmeg
Mixed herbs, thyme, bayleaf, parsley, or a bouquet garni

1. Mix together ingredients for the marinade and, several hours before cooking, put in meat.
2. Peel the onions and put in a pan with 25g/1oz, *(2 Tbsp)* butter or margarine. Add water to just cover. Cook gently, half-covered until the liquid is completely reduced. Put the raisins into a pan of cold water, place over gentle heat and bring to the boil. Draw pan off heat as soon as the water boils and allow the raisins to swell.
3. Drain the beef, reserving the marinade, and brown on all sides in 25g/1oz *(2 Tbsp)* butter or margarine. Remove beef and place in a roasting tin, pour over the fat from the pan. In the pan, pour ½ pint of the marinade, and ½ pint of beef stock made with the bouillon cube. Return to heat and stir well, then pour into the roasting tin. Put in a hot oven, Gas Mark 7, 425°F, 22°C. After 20 minutes, drain the raisins and add them, with the pre-cooked onions to the roasting tin. Season and return dish to oven for further 10 mins.
4. Remove from oven, and place meat on a hot serving dish. With a fork, mix together 1 teaspoon flour with the rest of the butter and add to the juices in the roasting tin. Boil for several minutes, stirring all the time with a wooden spoon. Serve the roast, cut in slices, with sauce poured over.

The Secret of white boiled rice: Add a few drops of lemon juice to the cooking water. White rice looks more appetizing, and makes the perfect accompaniment. Boil and drain in plenty of salted water, then press some into a tumbler with a wooden spoon. Up-turn the tumbler on to the serving dish and twist, and the rice will make a small 'timbale' or pyramid.

BÉARNAISE STEW

Preparation and cooking: 4 to 5 hours
In a pressure cooker: 1½ hours
Marinate overnight

For 8
2½kg/5lb stewing steak
200g/½lb belly of pork
1–2 tablespoons flour
300g/¾lb uncooked ham
Bouquet garni
1 small strong pimiento
Salt and pepper

The marinade
1 bottle red wine
2 tablespoons oil
Thyme and bay leaf
Pepper
2 onions
2 cloves
2 cloves garlic

1. Cut the steak into small cubes the evening before it is to be cooked. Marinate overnight in the marinade ingredients.
2. *Cooking*: Bring the belly of pork to the boil in water to cover, then drain it, score the skin and place in the bottom of a flameproof casserole. Drain the steak carefully and roll it in flour. Put it in the casserole with the raw ham, also diced. Then pour on the marinade with its spices, add the bouquet garni and the pimiento. Season with salt and pepper. Cover and leave to cook very gently for 4 to 5 hours (in a pressure cooker: 1 hour 30 minutes).

Boiled rice or plain boiled potatoes are the best vegetables to serve with a béarnaise stew.

Note: It is very unpleasant to find a pimiento served in the stew sauce. A good idea is to tie a long thread around it so that it can be easily removed before serving.

The Secret of a successful stew: It is the slow, regulated cooking which gives the meat its taste and tenderness. It is better to put the casserole in a slow oven (Gas Mark 3, 325°F, 155°C) rather than on top of the cooker. This helps prevent the meat sticking to the dish.

BEEF VIGNERONNE

Preparation and cooking: 3 hours
In a pressure cooker: 40 minutes

For 4
1½kg/2½lb stewing beef, cut in large pieces
3–4 tablespoons oil
100g/4oz (½ *cup*) butter or margarine
2 shallots, chopped
1 clove garlic
1 carrot, diced
Bouquet garni
2–3 heaped tablespoons flour
1 bottle rough red wine
12 button (pickling) onions, peeled
25g/1oz (*2 Tbsp*) extra butter (see method)
250g/8oz lean bacon
250g/8oz mushrooms
Salt and pepper

1. Quickly sauté the pieces of meat in a frypan or skillet in the hot oil. Heat half the butter in a large, separate pan and put in the meat. Add the chopped shallots, garlic, carrot, bouquet garni, salt and pepper and stir to mix. Sprinkle in the flour and cook over high heat until the flour is straw-coloured.
2. Pour the red wine over the meat. Cover the pan and allow to simmer for 2½ hours (in a pressure cooker: 40 minutes).
3. Meanwhile, cook the onions, with the chopped bacon in 25g/1oz *(2 Tbsp)* butter, if necessary. Add to the casserole 30 minutes before the end of the cooking time.
4. Clean, chop and sauté the mushrooms in the rest of the butter and add at the last minute. Serve with thick macaroni, with gravy poured over.

CHOOSING PORK

"From the pig, everything can be used."

Top quality pork can be recognized by:
—its pale pink flesh, which has a slightly pearly sheen
—its fine, close texture
—its very white, firm fat.

However, the exceptions are the back chops and the cuts for grilling (broiling), which should be deeper in colour and slacker in texture.

PORK CHOPS 'EN SAUPIQUET'

Preparation and cooking: 35 minutes

For 4
4 pork chops
30g/1½oz (3 *Tbsp*) butter or margarine
2 onions, finely chopped
6–7 tablespoons white wine vinegar
Fresh or dried thyme
½ a bay leaf
3 gherkins
1 tablespoon strong mustard
Salt and pepper

1. Quickly brown the chops on both sides in the butter over a high heat. Take them out of the pan and keep hot.
2. Put in the finely-chopped onions and cook over a moderate heat. When they are transparent sprinkle over the vinegar. Bring to the boil and boil for 1–2 minutes. Then add water, to halfway up the pan, salt, pepper, half a bay leaf and a sprig of thyme, or a pinch or two of dried thyme. Replace the meat, cover pan, and leave to simmer, covered, for 30 minutes.
3. Slice the gherkins into rounds and add them to the pan just before the end of the cooking time. Remove chops from the pan, drain and spread with mustard on both sides. Return to the pan and turn chops over a couple of times so the mustard melts into the cooking juices. Serve immediately without further cooking.

The Secret of a vinegar sauce which is not too acid: After adding all the vinegar boil the mixture fiercely, without a lid; this removes any excess acid taste and leaves only a slightly sharp flavour.

STUFFED PORK CUTLETS

Preparation and cooking: 45 minutes

For 4
4 lean pork cutlets (without bone)
200g/8oz sliced white bread
2 tablespoons thinly diced celery
3 (*4*) tablespoons milk
60g/2½oz (*4–5 Tbsp*) butter or margarine
A little flour
Salt and pepper

8–12 small skewers, or cocktail sticks

1. Pass the bread through a mincer (grinder) to make breadcrumbs. Place in a bowl with the celery, milk, salt, pepper and two-thirds of the butter or margarine. Bind all ingredients together into a smooth stuffing.
2. Slit the cutlets to form a pocket, and place a quarter of the stuffing in each (a). Close edges and secure with small skewers or cocktail sticks (*b*). Sprinkle with salt and pepper and dip into the flour.
3. Heat the remainder of the butter in a pan or skillet and brown the chops on both sides. Transfer from pan to a warmed gratin dish, cover the dish with foil and place in a moderate oven (Gas Mark 5, 375°F, 190°C) for 20 minutes.

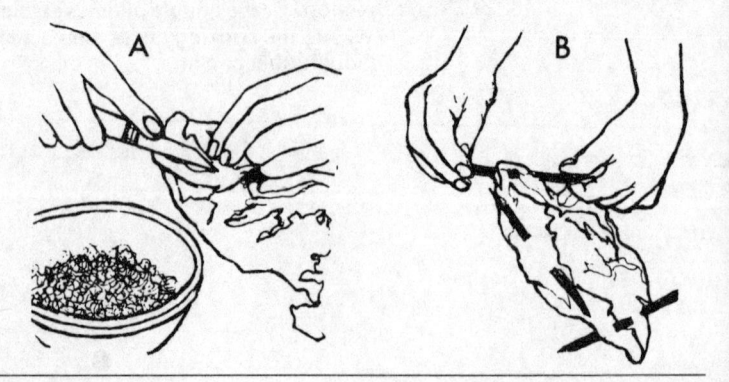

The Secret of keeping in the filling: Do not overfill each cutlet. Place a short skewer, or cocktail stick, at each end of the slit and one in the middle. This should do the trick.

PORK PAUPIETTES WITH FENNEL

Preparation and cooking: 1½ hours
In a pressure cooker: 25 minutes

For 4
1 kg/2lb pork fillet, cut into 4 portions
40g/1½–2oz (*3–4 Tbsp*) butter or margarine
1 fennel bulb
8 thin slices gruyère cheese
1 onion, sliced
1 carrot, diced
1 clove garlic, chopped
1 teaspoon flour
1 tomato, peeled and chopped
1 tablespoon tomato paste
Bouquet garni
⅓ glass of dry white wine
Salt and pepper

Fine string or thick kitchen thread

1. Well rinse and cut fennel into inch-thick rounds. On each portion of pork, place a slice of gruyère cheese, a round of fennel, a second slice of cheese and season with salt and pepper. Roll each fillet and tie up like a parcel with fine string.
2. In a flameproof casserole, brown the paupiettes in the butter or margarine. Add the rest of the ingredients, a glass of water and season with salt and pepper. Cover the casserole and allow to simmer over gentle heat for 1 hour, 10 minutes (in a pressure cooker: 25 minutes, use half the quantity of liquid). Serve with plain boiled noodles tossed in butter, or puréed potatoes.

Variation: You may find it easier to make 2 large paupiettes, and cut each in half when serving.

The Secret of a smooth, velvety sauce from simmered meat: Place a piece of pork fat, preferably blanched first (brought to the boil in cold water and drained) at the bottom of the casserole under the meat. This gradually helps the sauce achieve a really velvety smooth texture.

BRAISED PORK

Preparation and cooking: 1½ hours
In a pressure cooker: 40 minutes

For 4
1kg/2¼lb pork, boned, rolled and tied
30g/1½oz (*3 Tbsp*) butter or margarine
2 onions, quartered
2 tablespoons dry white wine
Bouquet garni
Salt and pepper

1. Heat the butter or margarine in a large flameproof casserole. Put in the joint and brown all over on a high heat.
2. Add the quartered onions and brown them in their turn. Then pour in the dry white wine and the same quantity of boiling water. Add the bouquet garni, salt and pepper. Cover and leave to cook gently for 1¼–1½ hours (in a pressure cooker: 40 minutes). Turn the meat over several times during cooking.

The Secret of a moist, well-braised joint: Quick browning on the outside seals in the juices before the slow cooking in the liquid. The joint should be allowed to cool completely before draining and slicing.

BRAISED PORK WITH ORANGE

Preparation and cooking: 2 hours

For 4
1½kg/3lb neck or loin of pork, on the bone
30g/1½oz (*2 Tbsp*) butter or margarine
1 onion, cut in rounds
1 carrot, diced
1 teaspoon tomato paste
2 cloves of garlic (peeled and halved)
1 glass dry white wine
Bouquet garni
4 oranges
1 liqueur glass Cointreau, or Grand Marnier, liqueur (optional)
Salt and pepper

1. In a large, flameproof casserole, brown the joint on all sides in the butter or margarine. Add the onion and carrot, tomato paste, garlic, white wine, bouquet garni and salt and pepper. Cover the casserole and allow to simmer over a low heat for 1 to 1¼ hours.
2. Peel the zest (orange-coloured surface, not the pith) of 2 oranges with a potato peeler, and cut into fine shreds. Put into a pan of cold water and bring to the boil. Boil for 2 minutes, then drain off the water, add the juice of 2 oranges to the pan, boil up for a few minutes.
3. Remove the meat from the casserole and keep hot. Strain the sauce, and return it to the casserole. Cook for 5 minutes with the shreds of zest, orange juice, and the glass of orange-flavoured liqueur if used.
4. Peel the other 2 oranges, cut flesh in rounds and serve the meat, surrounded with orange rounds and with the sauce poured over.

The Secret of achieving an orange flavour that is not too strong: Blanch the zest by putting it into cold water, then bringing it to the boil. When drained, the zest has lost its strong flavour, and will impart only a delicate flavour to the dish.

PORK GOULASH

Preparation and cooking: 1½ hours
In a pressure cooker: 25 minutes

For 4
1¼kg/2¼lb pork fillet, diced
50g/2oz (*4 Tbsp*) butter
4 onions, chopped
1-2 teaspoons paprika
4 tomatoes, skinned and sliced
4 tablespoon tomato paste
1 clove of garlic
Bouquet garni
800g/2lb potatoes
Salt and pepper

1. Brown the pieces of meat and chopped onion together in the butter, in a flameproof casserole. Add the paprika, the skinned and sliced tomatoes, tomato paste, crushed garlic, salt, pepper and bouquet garni. Half-fill the casserole with water, cover, and leave to cook gently in a slow oven (Gas Mark 3, 325°F, 160°C) for 40 minutes (in the pressure cooker: 12 to 15 minutes, with half the quantity of water).
2. Peel and quarter the potatoes and add them to the goulash. Leave dish to cook for a further 30 minutes (in the pressure cooker: 10 minutes).

The Secret of a thick rich-tasting goulash: Long, slow cooking in a slow oven, preferably in a cast iron casserole.

COUNTRY PORK STEW LIMOUSINE

Preparation and cooking: 2½ hours
In a pressure cooker: 1 hour

For 6–8
500g/1lb salt belly pork
200g/7–8oz slices of lean bacon
1 medium-size white cabbage, quartered
250g/½lb carrots, sliced
250g/½lb turnip, diced
250g/½lb leeks, sliced
2 cloves garlic
Bouquet garni
800g/2lb potatoes, roughly diced
4 pork chipolata sausages
Pepper

1. Put the quartered cabbage in boiling water in a deep casserole (pot-au-feu) and cook for 10 minutes. Drain.
2. Bring 4–5 pints water to the boil in the casserole, put in the salt belly pork, bacon, cabbage and the rest of the vegetables, except the potatoes. Add the garlic, bouquet garni and pepper. Do not add salt.
3. Allow to simmer on low for 2 hours (in a pressure cooker: 45 minutes).
4. Now add the potatoes, and leave stew to cook for a further 30 minutes (in a pressure cooker: 10 minutes) before serving.
5. Lightly sauté the chipolata sausages and serve with the stew.

The Secret of a savoury salt pork stew: Long, slow cooking, with no salt added. The pork is quite salty enough. If you find belly pork too salty, leave in cold water to cover for several hours, before draining and cooking. It may be necessary to do this more than once if the pork is very salty. (It should not be necessary to de-salt the pork for this recipe.)

VEAL & PORK PIE

Preparation and cooking: 1 hour 40 minutes Main course or starter
Marinate: preferably overnight

For 4–6
400g/14oz shoulder veal
200g/7oz pork fillet
A little beaten egg
2 egg yolks
Salt and pepper

The marinade
¼ litre/½ pint (1¼ *cups*) red wine
1 carrot, chopped
1 onion, chopped
1 shallot, chopped
Thyme, bay leaf
Parsley
Salt and pepper

The pastry
200g/7oz (1¾ *cups*) flour
100g/4oz (½ *cup*) butter or margarine
1 teaspoon salt

20 cm (9-inch) diameter flan dish

1. The evening before, put together the ingredients for the marinade, and place the meat in the dish.
2. *The pastry.* Rub the flour, butter and salt together with the palms of your hands until the mixture resembles fine breadcrumbs. Add just enough water (3 to 4 tablespoons) to make a smooth paste. Lightly knead into a ball, flatten out pastry, and knead again into a ball. Do this once more. Divide pastry into two, and roll out into rounds. Line the base of your flan dish with one.
3. Drain the meat, cut in cubes, season with salt and pepper, and place on the pastry base. Cover with the second pastry ring lightly dampened round the edges, and seal.
4. Cut out a hole in the centre of the crust and make a small pie funnel out of foil to slip inside to keep the hole open. Brush the surface of the pastry with a little beaten egg. Place in a hot oven (Gas Mark 6–7, 400°–425°F, 210°–220°C) for about an hour.
5. To ½-glass of the liquid from the marinade, add two egg yolks. Stir lightly and pour into the pie through the hole in the crust. Return to the oven for a further 5 minutes. Serve hot, with a green vegetable of your choice, or a mixed salad. It can be served, hot or cold, as a starter.

The Secret of a pie crust which does not split open during cooking: Do not moisten the edges of the pastry too thoroughly. Too much dampness prevents the pastry from sticking.

PORK ESCALOPES IN RED WINE

Preparation and cooking: 20 minutes

For 4
4 boneless pork cutlets, beaten thin
30g/1½oz (*3 Tbsp*) butter or margarine
1 shallot or small onion, chopped
2 tablespoons flour
1 teaspoon tomato paste
1 glass red wine
Chopped parsley
Salt and pepper

1. Cook the pork 'escalopes' in a frypan or skillet with half the butter or margarine for 4 minutes each side. Keep warm on a plate.
2. Replace the pan over gentle heat, put in the shallot to cook until transparent (without browning) in the rest of the butter or margarine. Sprinkle over the flour and stir to mix for a minute or two. Add tomato paste, wine, salt and pepper and bring to the boil, uncovered.
3. Replace the escalopes and cook for a further 5 minutes. Sprinkle with chopped parsley before serving. Serve with plain boiled potatoes, noodles or a purée of lentils.

The Secret of pork escalopes: If thin-cut fillets are hard to find, ask the butcher to remove bone and fat from thin-cut chops, and beat out until they are really thin. Less economical, but good, is pork fillet.

CHOOSING VEAL

Top quality veal can be recognized by:
– its very pale pink, slightly pearly flesh
– the fine grain of the flesh

SPIT ROAST VEAL

Preparation and cooking: 1¼ hours
To marinate: overnight

For 4
1kg/2½lb joint of veal for roasting, boned, rolled and tied
25g/1oz (*2 Tbsp*) butter
Rosemary (thyme or sage)
Salt and pepper

The marinade
1 onion, peeled and sliced
4 cloves
1 tablespoon oil
Thyme, bay leaf
1 glass dry white wine
Pepper

1. The night before cooking, marinate the meat in a pan just big enough to hold it and all the marinade ingredients. Cover and turn from time to time.
2. *Cooking.* Drain the meat, reserving the marinade. Slide sprigs of fresh rosemary or thyme under the string which ties it up. Stick firmly on spit to stop it becoming unbalanced. Season. Arrange spit at half-way height of rôtisserie or oven. The meat is cooked when it is golden-brown on the outside – in about 1 hour. If the meat is barded with fat (has strips of bacon fat threaded into the surface) skim the gravy before serving.

The Secret of a good spit roast: Brush with melted butter every 15 minutes while cooking and baste with marinade to flavour. Veal is very dry meat and strips of bacon fat threaded into the surface will help to make it succulent.

VEAL ESCALOPES IN BREADCRUMBS

Preparation and cooking: 20 minutes

For 4
4 thin veal escalopes
40g/1½oz (*3 Tbsp*) butter or margarine
2 tablespoons flour
2 eggs, beaten
2 (*1½*) cups golden breadcrumbs
Slices of lemon
Salt and pepper

1. Take three plates. Put the measured flour on one, the beaten eggs on the second, and the breadcrumbs on the third. Coat the escalopes firstly with the flour, then the egg, then the breadcrumbs. Press down the breadcrumbs with the flat side of a knife to ensure that they stick.
2. Melt the butter or margarine in a medium-hot frypan or skillet, then cook the escalopes for 5 minutes each side. Garnish each with a slice or two of lemon.

Organization: The frypan or skillet will probably be too small, so cook the escalopes two at a time. Keep the first two hot and use a little extra butter for each frying, otherwise the breadcrumb coating will absorb a lot of butter and may burn.

Variation: Serve each escalope garnished with some capers, a little chopped, hard-boiled egg, an olive wrapped in an anchovy fillet and a sprinkling of chopped parsley, and you have a Wiener Schnitzel. Serve with lemon wedges, grilled (broiled) tomatoes and spinach.

The Secret of frying escalopes that do not split away from the coating when taken out of the pan: They should be well-coated all over in egg and flour and, above all, do not be sparing with the breadcrumbs. Pour them on liberally and thoroughly coat the escalopes. They can be left in a refrigerator for about an hour between coating and cooking to ensure the best results.

VEAL ESCALOPES WITH ORANGE

Preparation and cooking: 20 minutes

For 4
4 veal escalopes
1 tablespoon flour
40g/1½oz (*3 Tbsp*) butter or margarine
Juice of 2 oranges
Salt and pepper

1. Dip the escalopes in seasoned flour. Lightly brown them in a pan with three-quarters of the butter or margarine – cooking for only 4 minutes on each side.
2. During cooking, sprinkle the meat from time to time with the fresh orange juice mixed with 2 tablespoons of water. Cover and leave to simmer for a further 5 minutes.
3. Turn out the escalopes on to a hot dish. Add the rest of the butter to any juices remaining in the pan on the heat and stir vigorously with a wooden spoon. Pour immediately over the escalopes.

Plain boiled rice makes the best accompaniment to this dish (*see page 172*).

Optional extra: For a nicely garnished dish, finely shred the orange zest and arrange a pinch on each escalope.

The Secret of veal escalopes which don't curl up on cooking: Make a few little cuts round the edges with the point of a knife or scissors before coating. This way, they should stay flat.

VEAL CUTLETS 'EN PAPILLOTE'

Preparation and cooking: 1 hour

For 4
4 thin veal cutlets
600g/1¼lb large flat mushrooms
2 tablespoons vinegar
1 tablespoon oil
60g/2½oz (5 Tbsp) butter or margarine
4 tablespoons dry white wine
Salt and pepper

1. Slit the base of the mushroom stalks, wash them quickly but thoroughly, in water with 2 tablespoons vinegar. Drain them by squeezing between the hands. Put them in a large pan with the oil and cook gently for 5 minutes until they have released their juices, then drain.
2. Brown the cutlets in a large pan, in three-quarters of the butter or margarine. Remove from the pan, and fry the mushrooms with salt, pepper and white wine for 5 to 6 minutes over a high heat.
3. Cut four large triangular pieces of kitchen foil or waxed paper and place one cutlet on each, with a quarter of the mushrooms and one or two dots of butter. Fold the paper over the cutlet and mushrooms and seal the edges completely. Cook in a hot oven (Gas Mark 7, 425°F, 220°C) for 20 minutes and serve in the paper or foil.

The Secret of meat 'en papillote' giving plenty of room to swell: The triangle-shape should be cut very large so that the meat is not compressed too tightly. Leave an extra margin of 2–3 cm. (about 1–1½ in) around the cutlet sides so that the paper, or foil, will not stick to the meat and will be able to puff up, away from the chop while cooking.

PAUPIETTES OF VEAL CORDON BLEU

Preparation and cooking: 1 hour

For 4
4 large thin veal escalopes
50g/2oz (*4 Tbsp*) butter or margarine
2 slices cooked ham
1 tablespoon English made mustard
4 slices gruyère cheese
Salt and pepper

The coating
2 eggs, beaten
2 tablespoons flour
Breadcrumbs

1. Season the escalopes with salt and pepper. Arrange half a slice of ham spread with mustard, and a slice of gruyère cheese on each one. Roll up, folding in the sides like a parcel to hold the filling (*a*). Tie crosswise with string (*b*).
2. Roll the paupiettes in the beaten egg, then the flour and finally the breadcrumbs. They should be completely coated.
3. Cook, covered, in a pan or skillet with the butter or margarine over a moderate heat for 30 to 40 minutes (or better still in a moderate oven, Gas Mark 4, 350°F, 180°C). Serve with potato croquettes (*see page 184*).

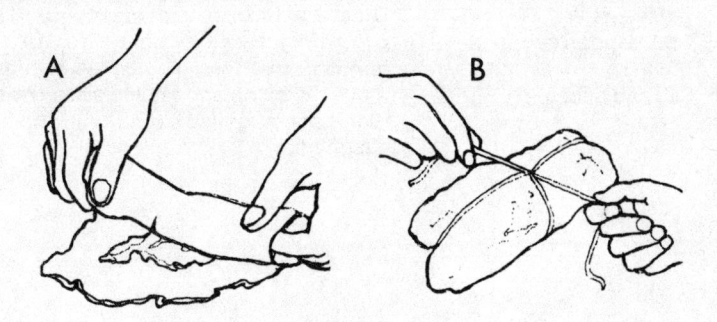

The Secret of succulent, well-shaped paupiettes: Put them in the pre-set moderate oven half-way through cooking to finish off.

PAUPIETTES OF VEAL PROVENÇAL

Preparation and cooking: 1 hour
In a pressure cooker: 20 minutes

For 4
4 veal escalopes
50g/2oz (*4 Tbsp*) butter or margarine
1 large piece pork or bacon fat, cut in four strips
100g/4oz (*1 cup*) stoned green olives
Salt and pepper

The stuffing
100g/4oz fresh white bread
4 tablespoons milk
100g/4oz (*1¼ cups*) mushrooms
1 clove garlic
1 tablespoon chopped parsley
Salt and pepper

1. *The stuffing.* Crumble bread into a bowl and soak in the milk. Trim and rinse mushrooms. Chop them with the garlic and parsley. Drain and squeeze bread to remove excess liquid. Spoon into the mushroom mixture and season, pressing well together.
2. Spread a quarter of the stuffing on each escalope. Fold each in four. Wrap a strip of fat round each and tie up with string like a parcel to hold in the stuffing.
3. Melt the butter or margarine in a fry pan or skillet and lightly brown the paupiettes all over. Season, cover, and leave to simmer over low heat for 30 minutes (in a pressure cooker: 12 minutes).
4. Boil the olives in a pan of water for 5 minutes. Drain and rinse in cold water. Add to the pan of paupiettes. Leave to simmer for a further 5–10 minutes (in a pressure cooker: 5 minutes). Remove the string and fat and serve the paupiettes with plain grilled (broiled) tomatoes and spaghetti.

The Secret of paupiettes that are easy to fill: Buy wide, very thin escalopes of veal and get the butcher to flatten them as much as possible for you, or flatten them yourself by beating out with a cutlet bat.

VEAL CHOPS VALLÉE D'AUGE

Preparation and cooking: 30 minutes

For 4
4 veal chops
30g/1½oz (*3 Tbsp*) butter or margarine
8–10 button onions
250g/8oz mushrooms
2–3 tablespoons flour
2 liqueur glasses Calvados (apple brandy)
4 tablespoons thick cream
Salt and pepper

1. Peel the onions. Cook them for 5 minutes in boiling water and then drain. Clean and chop the mushrooms.
2. Season the veal chops with salt and pepper and coat them in flour. Melt the butter or margarine in a large pan and slowly brown the chops on each side. Add the onions and mushrooms and simmer for 20 minutes, covering the pan for the last 10 minutes.
3. When cooked, add the Calvados, bring to the boil and set alight. Remove the meat and pour the cream into the Calvados sauce in the pan. Boil for a couple of seconds, stirring continuously with a wooden spoon. Adjust the seasoning, then pour over the chops and serve with plain boiled potatoes, pasta or rice, all of which go particularly well with the rich cream sauce.

The Secret of successful flaming: Heat up the spirit (Calvados or brandy) to be flamed before setting alight and make sure in savoury dishes, that there is not too much liquid in the pan. Otherwise it will dilute the spirit and it will not flame.

VEAL CUTLETS NORMANDE

Preparation and cooking: 25 minutes

For 4
4 veal escalopes
30g/1½oz (*3 Tbsp*) butter or margarine
½ glass dry white wine
Fresh tarragon
1 tablespoon flour
3 tablespoons thick cream
Salt and pepper

Baked apples for serving

1. Brown the escalopes in a pan of hot margarine or butter for 3–4 minutes on each side. Add the white wine and tarragon stalks, keeping the leaves for later use. Cover and leave to simmer for 10 minutes.
2. Put the cooked escalopes on a plate and keep them hot, leaving the wine and cooking juices in the pan. Add one or two tablespoons of water and bring to the boil for one minute. Remove the tarragon stalks. Now add the cream and chopped tarragon leaves to the pan, bringing the sauce back to the boil, for one minute. Pour the sauce over the escalopes and serve with baked apples.

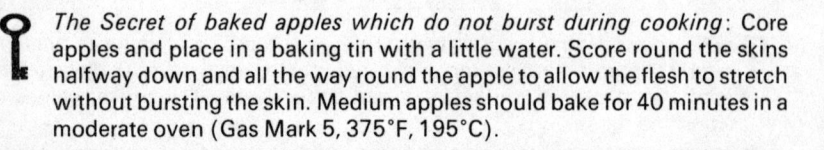

The Secret of baked apples which do not burst during cooking: Core apples and place in a baking tin with a little water. Score round the skins halfway down and all the way round the apple to allow the flesh to stretch without bursting the skin. Medium apples should bake for 40 minutes in a moderate oven (Gas Mark 5, 375°F, 195°C).

BREAST OF VEAL PAYSANNE

Preparation and cooking: 2 hours 30 minutes
In a pressure cooker: 35 minutes

For 4
1½kg/3lb breast of veal, cut in pieces
200g/½lb bacon, preferably streaky
4 carrots
2 turnips
1 onion, stuck with a clove
1 clove garlic
Bouquet garni
1 cabbage heart
Salt and pepper

The sauce
1 tablespoon flour
25g/1oz (*2 Tbsp*) butter or margarine
Juice of ½ a lemon
1 tablespoon fresh cream *or* one egg yolk
1 pickled gherkin
1 tablespoon chopped parsley

1. Put the veal pieces and bacon in a saucepan of unsalted water. Bring slowly to the boil and immediately pour off the liquid into a bowl to remove any scum which may form during cooking. Skim, and keep the liquid on one side.
2. Return the pan to the heat. Add just enough boiling water to cover the meat. Add peeled carrots, peeled and quartered turnips, onion stuck with a clove, garlic, bouquet garni, salt and pepper.
3. Wash and quarter the cabbage heart. Make a cut in the stalk at the base and cook in boiling water for 5 minutes. Drain, then add to the pan with the veal, bacon and the rest of the vegetables. Cover and simmer for 1 hour 30 minutes (in a pressure cooker: 30 minutes).
4. *The sauce*: Mix the margarine or butter with the flour and ½ pint (*1¼ cups*) of the stock from the meat. Stir with a sauce whisk over a low heat until it starts to boil. Leave to simmer for 5 minutes, then strain the meat and vegetables thoroughly and place in a deep serving dish. Serve the sauce separately.

The Secret of thickening the sauce correctly: Squeeze the lemon juice into a bowl with the egg yolk or fresh cream, the sliced gherkin and 1 tablespoon chopped parsley. Stir this briskly into the sauce for a few seconds over a low heat. Remove from the heat immediately, and pour into a sauceboat.

BLANQUETTE OF VEAL À L'ANCIENNE

Preparation and cooking: 1¾ hours
In a pressure cooker: 40 minutes

For 4
1kg/2¼lb boned shoulder veal, cut into large cubes
40g/1½oz (*3 Tbsp*) butter or margarine
1 carrot, sliced
1 onion, sliced
2 tablespoons flour
Bouquet garni
2 cloves
Chopped parsley
Salt and pepper

The thickening
1 egg yolk
2 tablespoons thick cream

1. Lightly brown the meat with the butter or margarine and the sliced carrot and onion. Dust with the flour and stir well so that the flour is lightly cooked.
2. Add ½ litre/¾ pint, (*1 pint*) hot water, the bouquet garni, cloves, salt and pepper and cook over a low heat for about 1¼ hours (in a pressure cooker: 25 minutes).
3. When the meat is cooked, drain carefully and keep hot on a serving dish. Leave the pan, uncovered, on the heat, to allow the sauce to reduce. Remove the carrot and the bouquet garni.
4. *The thickening.* In a large bowl, mix together the egg yolk and cream. Gradually add the hot sauce from the pan, stirring continuously with a sauce whisk or wooden spoon. Pour the thickened sauce over the meat. Dust with a little chopped parsley, and serve immediately with plain boiled potatoes or rice.

Variation: Add 226g (8oz) button mushrooms, softened in a little butter, about 15 minutes before the end of the cooking time (in a pressure cooker: 5 minutes).

The Secret of thickening a blanquette: 1–2 spoonfuls of the very hot sauce are added to the bowl of egg and cream (not the other way round) while whisking all the time, then this is blended into the rest of the sauce over a low heat. If the blanquette has to wait before serving, it must be kept in the oven in a bain-marie (a roasting tin half-full of hot water).

VEAL SAUTÉ MENTONNAISE

Preparation and cooking: 2 hours 15 minutes
In a pressure cooker: 45 minutes

For 4
1½kg/3lb stewing or boneless shoulder veal, cut into eight pieces
100g/4oz (*1 cup*) stoned green olives
500g/1lb tomatoes
40g/2oz (*4 Tbsp*) butter or margarine
1 level tablespoon flour
1 onion, sliced
1 clove
2 cloves garlic
Bouquet garni
1 glass dry white wine
Chopped parsley
Salt and pepper

1. Put the olives in cold water and bring them gently to the boil. Strain them and rinse thoroughly in cold water to remove any bitter taste. Skin the tomatoes, halve them and remove the pips and juice so that only the pulp is used.
2. Lightly cook the meat in a saucepan with the butter or margarine. Sprinkle with the flour and mix this with the butter over high heat. Add the tomato pulp, onion, clove, garlic, bouquet garni, white wine, a pinch of salt and a fair sprinkling of pepper. Cover and simmer for 1¾ hours (in a pressure cooker: 35 minutes).
3. Sprinkle the chopped parsley on the meat just before serving with boiled rice or buttered pasta.

The Secret of making a sauté with fresh tomatoes which blend fully with the other ingredients: The tomatoes should be just ripe and have all the liquid and pips removed. To do this they have to be peeled and quartered. If you do not like to waste the pips, skin and centres, they can be kept for a soup.

VEAL MARENGO

Preparation and cooking: 1 hour 50 minutes
In a pressure cooker: 35 minutes

For 4
1kg/2¼lb pieces of boned shoulder veal
40g/1½oz (*3 Tbsp*) butter or margarine
3 shallots
1 carrot, chopped
1 tablespoon flour
2 tablespoons tomato paste
¼ litre/½ pint (1¼ *cups*) dry white wine
2 cloves of garlic
Bouquet garni
125g/4–5oz (1¼ *cups*) mushrooms
Salt and pepper

1. Brown the meat all over in the melted butter or margarine in a flameproof casserole. Then add the shallots and chopped carrots. Sprinkle on the flour and mix in well with the butter.
2. Now add the tomato paste, white wine, an equal quantity of water, the garlic, bouquet garni, and season with salt and pepper. Cover and simmer over a low heat for 1½ hours (in a pressure cooker: 30 minutes).
3. Meanwhile, split the ends of the mushroom stalks, wash them, and cut into thin strips. Add them to the casserole, cover, and cook for a further 15 minutes (in a pressure cooker: 5 minutes). Serve with plain boiled or creamed potatoes.

The Secret of a good Marengo: If, when cooked, the marengo sauce doesn't look thick enough, remove the pieces of meat and boil up the sauce, uncovered, for a few minutes to reduce and thicken. When in season a few peeled and quartered fresh tomatoes can be added, but a little tomato purée is still needed to give the right flavour.

CHOOSING LAMB AND MUTTON

Top quality lamb and mutton can be recognized by:
– its soft to dark red coloured flesh
– its size (they vary in size, but the best are small)
– a reasonable covering of firm white fat

ROAST LEG OF LAMB

Preparation and cooking: 40–50 minutes

For 6
1–2kg/2–4lb leg of lamb, or 1 rolled, boned shoulder weighing 1½kg/3lb

1. Pre-heat the oven (very hot).
2. Slide pieces of garlic between the meat and the bone or between the fat and the meat. Season with salt and pepper. Place in a large roasting tin and put in the pre-set oven. (A leg takes 35 minutes, a shoulder takes 45 minutes).
3. Baste occasionally while cooking. When cooked, turn off the oven, leaving the meat in for about 10 minutes.

The Secret of a leg or other roast of lamb which stays hot in the middle and is easy to slice: it should be left for 15 to 30 minutes before being carved. This allows the fibres of the meat to relax and the heat and blood to be distributed evenly throughout the joint. While waiting to carve, cover the meat in 2 or 3 thicknesses of aluminium foil to retain the heat.

BRAISED SHOULDER WITH HERB STUFFING

Preparation and cooking: 1¼ hours

For 4–6
1 shoulder of lamb, boned, weighing about 1kg/2¼lb
1–2 glasses dry white wine
A few sprigs of fresh thyme, if available
1 tablespoon oil

The stuffing
The following dried herbs: Thyme, rosemary, oregano, basil (optional)
50g/2oz (*4 Tbsp*) butter
Chopped fresh parsley
2 cloves garlic
1 egg
Salt and pepper

1. Set the oven at Gas Mark 8, 450°F, 230°C. Make the stuffing: Work the chopped parsley into the butter with a fork. Chop the garlic and work it into the parsley butter, then add the egg, salt and pepper and a good pinch of thyme, rosemary, oregano and basil. Mix well.
2. Spread this herb butter on the inside of the shoulder, roll up and tuck in the ends to hold in the stuffing. Tie up with fine string at intervals of 1–1½ inches along its length, place on a roasting dish, garnished with sprigs of thyme. Sprinkle over oil.
3. Place in the pre-set hot oven, and leave to cook for 10–12 minutes. Turn the joint over during this time. When it is nicely browned, take out, drain off any excess fat and return to the oven. Baste with a glass or two of dry white wine. Turn down the oven to Gas Mark 5, 375°F, 190°C, for a further 45 minutes. Baste often during cooking.
4. Serve the meat, cut in slices, with the cooking juices handed separately.

Suitable vegetables to accompany – green beans, fennel, celery or plain boiled potatoes.

Variation: This stuffed shoulder can also be cooked on a spit. In this case, it should be brushed over several times with a clean pastry brush soaked in dry white wine during cooking.

Fresh tarragon, also, can be used in season.

The Secret of succulent braised lamb: Quick cooking at the start to seal in the juices. Lamb is a greasy meat, and the wine counteracts excess fattiness – and saves indigestion.

BREAST OF MUTTON

Preparation and cooking: 1¼ hours

For 4
1 breast of lamb or mutton, boned, weighing about 1kg/2–2½lb
½ glass hot milk
50g/2oz (*1–2 slices*) bread
1 egg
60g/2½oz (*5 Tbsp*) butter or margarine
1kg/2lb 2oz fresh spinach
Salt and pepper

Trussing needle and fine string

1. Remove stalks and wash spinach. Cook in boiling water for 5 minutes. Drain well and roughly chop.
2. Pour the hot milk on to the bread in a large bowl. Add the egg and season with salt and pepper. Melt half the butter in a pan and add to the egg mixture. Mash all the ingredients together and lastly, work in the spinach. Pack this stuffing tightly into the cavity inside the breast of lamb (*a*). Sew up the breast with a trussing needle and string (*b*).
3. Put the meat in a roasting dish. Spread lightly with the remaining butter or margarine and season it. Cook in a moderate oven (Gas Mark 5, 375°F, 190°C) for 45 minutes. Halfway through the cooking, baste the meat and add one glass of hot water. When carving the joint, use a very sharp knife and do not squeeze the meat or the soft stuffing will fall out (*c*).

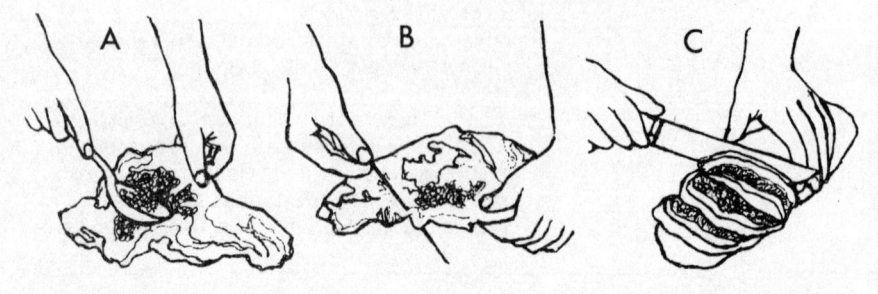

The Secret of carving stuffed meat: Leave it to stand for a few moments after removing from the oven before carving, or the stuffing may collapse.

LAMB CUTLETS CHAMPVALLON

Preparation and cooking: 1 hour

For 4
4 cutlets of lamb, trimmed of fat
30g/1½oz (*3 Tbsp*) butter or margarine
2 large onions
1kg/2¼lb potatoes
2 cloves garlic
Bouquet garni
1 stock cube
Salt and pepper

1. Peel and slice onions and potatoes.
2. Season the cutlets. Lightly brown them on both sides in the butter or margarine, then remove and put in the potato and onions to quickly sauté.
3. Arrange half the potatoes and onions in a shallow casserole dish. Place the cutlets on top, with the garlic and bouquet garni. Cover with the remaining potatoes and onions. Dissolve the stock cube in ½ litre (1 pint, *1¼ cups*) warm water, and pour into the casserole dish to come halfway up the sides. Cover and cook in a moderate oven (Gas Mark 5, 375°F, 190°C) for 30 to 40 minutes.

The Secret of perfect cutlets Champvallon: You start to cook them on top of the stove, and finish off in a moderate oven. They take a little longer to cook through.

LAMB CUTLETS MILANAISE

Preparation and cooking: 30 minutes

For 4
4 or 8 lamb cutlets (ask the butcher to flatten them for you)
50g/2oz ($\frac{1}{2}$ *cup*) grated gruyère or parmesan cheese
6 tablespoons fresh white breadcrumbs
3 tablespoons flour
1 or 2 eggs, beaten
30g/1$\frac{1}{2}$oz (*3 Tbsp*) butter or margarine
1 lemon
Salt and pepper

1. Mix together the grated cheese and breadcrumbs. Season the lamb cutlets and dip them first in the flour then the beaten egg and lastly in the cheese and breadcrumb mixture. Press down the breadcrumb mixture with the flat side of a knife so that it sticks to the cutlets.
2. Melt the butter or margarine in a large frypan or skillet and fry the cutlets over medium heat for about 3 minutes on each side, by which time they should be golden brown. Serve with lemon quarters.

Serve this dish with spaghetti; courgettes (zucchini); aubergines (egg plants); or tomatoes fried with garlic and parsley; green beans; garden peas or even button mushrooms.

The Secret of frying lamb cutlets without the coating splitting off during cooking: Do not be sparing with the beaten egg and cheese and breadcrumb mixture. Add a little more if your cutlets are large and use 2 eggs.

BLANQUETTE OF LAMB

Preparation and cooking: 1 hour 40 minutes
In a pressure cooker: 45 minutes

For 4
1kg/2¼lb neck or breast of lamb
¼ litre/½ pint (1¼ *cups*) dry white wine
1 onion, chopped
2 cloves
1 carrot, chopped
1 clove garlic, chopped
Bouquet garni

The sauce
30g/1½oz (*2–3 Tbsp*) butter or margarine
1 tablespoon flour
2–3 cups cooking liquid (see method)
1 egg yolk
Juice of ½ lemon
Chopped parsley
Salt and pepper

1. Bring a pan of water to the boil, put in the meat and allow to boil for 2 minutes. Drain, rinse under the tap and put the meat into a flameproof casserole with the white wine, onion, cloves, carrot, garlic, and bouquet garni. Season with salt and pepper. Add enough water to cover the meat, then cover and simmer for 1 hour (in a pressure cooker: 40 minutes).
2. *The sauce.* Over a low heat, mix the butter or margarine with the flour. Add 2 cups of the liquid from the meat and stir until boiling. Remove meat from casserole and drain. Add the drained pieces of meat to the sauce and leave to simmer together for about ¼ hour.
3. In a bowl, mix the egg yolk and lemon juice, using a sauce whisk. Whisk a few spoonfuls of the sauce from the meat into this mixture before pouring this liaison (thickening) back into the stew. Mix well and sprinkle with chopped parsley before serving.

The Secret of a blanquette of lamb which doesn't taste like old mutton: It's all in the short blanching in boiling water of the meat at the start, followed by rinsing under the tap. This removes strong flavours.

LEG OF LAMB BOULANGÈRE

Preparation and cooking: 1¼ hours

For 8
1 leg of lamb weighing about 2kg/5lb
50g/2oz (*4 Tbsp*) butter or margarine
250g/9oz onions
1½kg/3lb potatoes
Bouquet garni
Salt and pepper

1. Lightly brown the leg of lamb on all sides in a large pan in half the butter or margarine. Then, without adding extra fat, put the meat into a hot oven (Gas Mark 7–8, 425–450°F, 220–230°C) for 10 minutes.
2. Slice the onions into rings and soften them in the rest of the butter over a low heat. Thinly slice the potatoes.
3. Remove the lamb from the oven and arrange the potatoes and onions on the bottom of the baking dish. Add the bouquet garni, salt, pepper and enough boiling water to just cover the potatoes. Replace the lamb and cook for at least a further 35 minutes. Turn off the oven and allow the meat to 'rest' for 10 minutes before serving.

The Secret of succulent lamb Boulangère: The lamb is first browned to seal in the juices, then 'French roasted' in a little water, which keeps the meat moist.

QUICK MOUSSAKA

Preparation and cooking: 1 hour 30 minutes

Moussaka, of Roumanian origin, is an excellent dish of aubergines (egg plants), mutton and mushrooms, flavoured with herbs and spices. However, if made the traditional way, its preparation involves considerable care. For this recipe, the more complicated method has been sacrificed for a simpler way, which loses none of the dish's traditional character.

For 4
- 400g/1lb boned mutton (lamb), raw or cooked
- 1 shallot
- Parsley
- 100g/4oz ($1\frac{1}{4}$ cups) mushrooms
- 2 tomatoes
- 1 onion
- 4 cloves garlic
- 1 egg, beaten
- 1kg/$2\frac{1}{2}$lb aubergines (egg plants)
- A little flour
- Salt and pepper
- Olive oil for frying

1. Chop the mutton, shallot and half the parsley. Clean the mushrooms and skin the tomatoes. Halve tomatoes and squeeze out pips and juice.
2. Finely chop the onion and cook in 2 tablespoons olive oil until transparent, in a flameproof casserole. Add the chopped meat and allow to cook for an instant over a high heat. Add the mushrooms, the tomatoes, cut in slices, the crushed garlic, salt and pepper and stir all the ingredients until mixed. Leave to cook on a moderate heat for 15 minutes, stirring regularly. Remove from the heat and add the beaten egg.
3. Slice the aubergines (egg plants) into rounds without skinning them. Coat them in flour and fry in several tablespoons of olive oil for one or two minutes each side. Season with salt and pepper.
4. Using a deep-sided baking or soufflé dish, arrange the ingredients in layers, starting with aubergines, then meat mixture, then aubergines and continue until the dish is filled. Place the soufflé dish in a roasting tin half-filled with hot water. Cook, in this 'bain marie', in a hot oven (Gas Mark 7, 425°F, 220°C) for 45 minutes to an hour. Serve with a little parsley sprinkled on top.

The Secret of peeling tomatoes quickly whether ripe or not: Slip them into a pan of water which is just coming to the boil. Allow to boil, then drain immediately and peel right away. This method is particularly good for tomatoes to be used in cooking.

DOLMAS

Preparation and cooking: 2 hours
In a pressure cooker: ¾ hour

Main course or starter

For 4–6
1kg/2¼lb shoulder of lamb with bone
60g/½oz (*generous ⅓ cup*) rice
30g/1½oz (*3 Tbsp*) butter or margarine
1 medium-size green cabbage
8 cloves garlic
50g/2oz stoned black olives
Cayenne pepper
1 large can tomato purée, or 1 large can Italian tomatoes
Salt and pepper

1. Mince (grind) the meat, keeping the bone to one side. Wash the rice, add it, uncooked, to the minced (ground) meat and bind together with an egg yolk. Season with salt and pepper, a pinch of cayenne and add half the butter.
2. Take eight or so of the largest outer cabbage leaves and put them in boiling salted water for two minutes. Remove the toughest part of the stalk.
3. Put the bone to cook with half the butter or margarine in a large saucepan.
4. Place one tablespoon of stuffing and 1 or 2 peeled cloves of garlic (according to taste) on each softened cabbage leaf. Roll it up like a tobacco leaf round a cigar, turning in the ends so the filling is completely enclosed. Tie up the leaves with very fine string. Arrange the leaves in the saucepan with the meat bone. Finally, cover with tomato purée or canned tomatoes, and simmer for 1 hour 30 minutes (in a pressure cooker: 45 minutes). Add the black olives towards the end of cooking, allowing just enough time for them to heat through. Remove string before serving, and hand any tomato sauce separately. Dolmas can be served as a main course or as a starter.

The Secret of tasty Dolmas: If you cook the olives for longer, they will flavour the sauce with a strong, bitter taste. Add a little water if the tomato purée reduces too much.

WINDSOR PIE

Preparation and cooking: 1½ hours

For 4
300g/10oz boned shoulder of lamb
1 onion
75g/3oz cooked ham
1 egg, beaten
Chopped thyme
Salt and pepper

The shortcrust pastry
150g/6oz (1½ *cups*) flour
75g/3oz (⅓ *cup*) butter or margarine
½ teaspoon salt
Milk or water to brush pastry

17 cm (7–8 in) diameter pie dish

1. *Make the shortcrust pastry*: Mix together the flour, salt and fat, rubbing the mixture between the palms of your hands until the mixture looks like fine breadcrumbs. Add 3 to 4 tablespoons water gradually, just enough to knead mixture to a firm paste. Roll into a ball. Knock down with the palm of your hand and roll up again. Do this twice more.
2. Mince (grind) the meat, onion and ham together. Mix well with the egg, thyme, salt and pepper. Roll out the pastry into 2 rounds a little larger than the pie dish. Line one piece into the dish and prick with a fork (*a*). Fill with meat mixture. Lightly moisten the edges of the pastry (*b*) and arrange the second layer of pastry on top (*c*). Trim the top layer to fit (*d*), pinch the edges together (*e*), and then brush surface with milk or water. Bake in the oven at Gas Mark 6, 400°F, 210°C, for 50 minutes. Serve with a green vegetable, or salad, of your choice.

The Secret of a pie which cooks through: Use a pastry funnel, or cut a hole in the top of the pastry to allow the steam to escape during cooking.

A

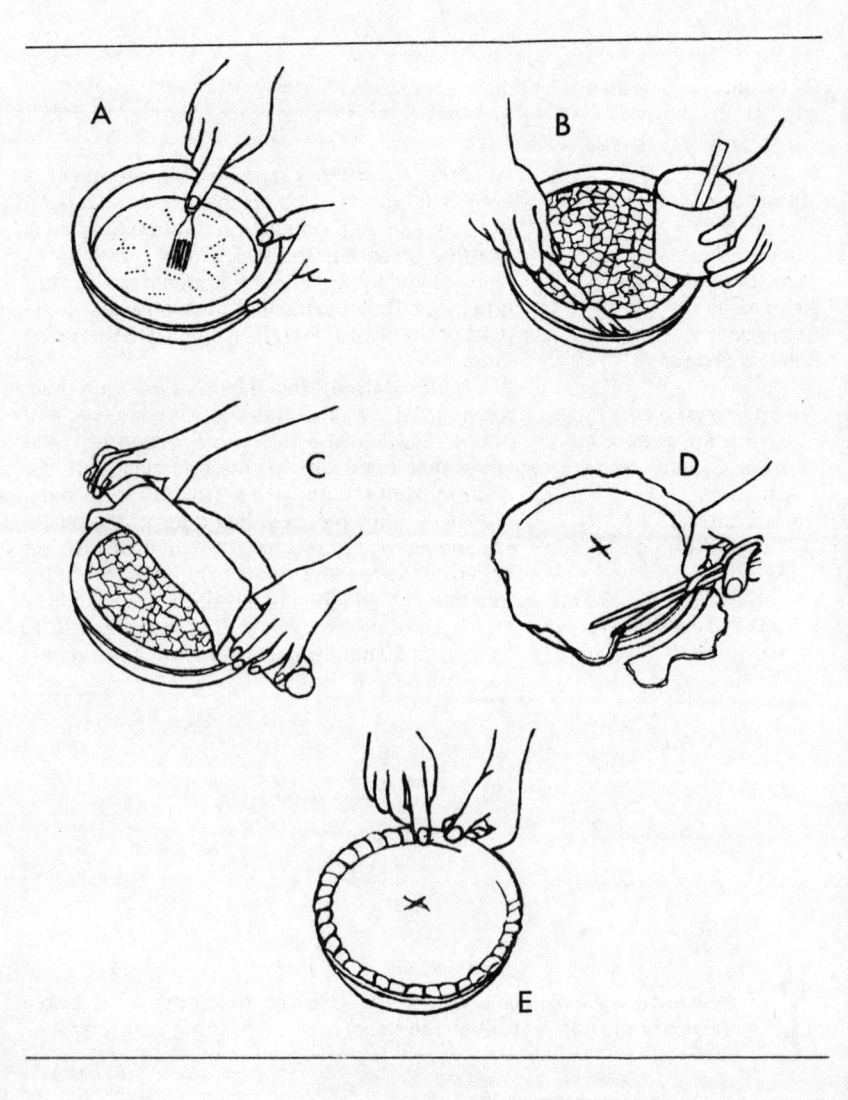

B

C

D

E

MARINADES FOR MEAT & GAME

MARINADE MIXTURE

For 1 bottle of red or white wine use:
½ glass wine vinegar
3 tablespoons oil
1 small carrot, chopped
1 onion, chopped
1–2 shallots, cut in rings
1 small stick of celery
1 clove garlic
1 stalk parsley
1 sprig thyme
1 bay leaf
3 peppercorns
1 clove

Put the meat or game in a container just big enough to hold it and the other ingredients. Add all the marinade ingredients and leave to marinate (soak) in a cool place for one to two days in summer and 3 to 4 days in winter. Turn the meat regularly.

Variation: Cooking is usually used to save time in marinating. Use the same ingredients as above but slightly brown the onions, carrot and chopped shallot in a tablespoon of oil. Then add the rest of the ingredients and simmer for 30 minutes. Allow to cool completely before pouring over the meat. Marinate overnight in summer, 2 days in winter.

QUICK MARINADE

(for small pieces of meat or game; steaks, cutlets escalopes, etc)
½ glass oil
Juice of ½ lemon
Sprig thyme
Bay leaf
Small sprig fennel (optional)
Salt and pepper

Leave meat to marinate in these ingredients for ½ hour at least, turning at least once.

The Secrets of marinating: Only pure wine vinegar should be used. The oil keeps in the various flavours by protecting the spices from the air.
Only a very little salt should be used, if any at all.
White wine masks the flavour of the meat less than red wine.
Marinating in red wine, on the other hand, gives more taste and substance to the sauce.
The meat should be turned several times in the marinade.

CHOOSING OFFAL (Variety Meats)

Offal can be the dearest of meats if you go for delicacies such as calves' sweetbreads, or the most economical if you enjoy tripe or calves' feet. The most important thing is that offal must be fresh. Nutritionists will tell you that it is rich in protein, iron, fats and the vitamins A, B and C. These recipes should convince you that these 'variety meats' can be tasty too.

Liver – needs no preparation before cooking, except for rinsing. The cheaper types, eg ox liver, can be 'tenderised' by soaking in milk for an hour before cooking.

Kidneys – must have the skin removed before cooking, and the white core must also be cut away from the centre.

Brains – should be soaked for some hours in cold, salted water before cooking, then blanched by bringing to the boil in fresh water and drained and rinsed under cold water.

Sweetbreads – should also be soaked for several hours in salted water to which two tablespoons of vinegar may be added. Blanch as for brains, above, before removing any ducts and skin.

Tripe – merely needs rinsing well in cold water with a tablespoon of vinegar added before cooking.

LIVER WITH ANCHOVY

Preparation and cooking: 20 minutes

For 4
4 slices lamb's, pig's or ox liver
30g/1½oz (*3 Tbsp*) butter or margarine
2 anchovy fillets, or 1 tablespoon anchovy paste
1 tablespoon chopped fresh mixed herbs or ½ teaspoon dried mixed herbs
A little flour
1 lemon
Pepper

1. Soak the anchovy fillets well in warm water to remove excess saltiness. Chop, then pound to a paste with a wooden spoon.
2. Melt the butter or margarine in a pan and add the anchovy paste and herbs, and cook gently for 3–4 minutes.
3. Dip the liver slices in flour, and add to the pan. Allow to cook for 3 minutes on each side over gentle heat. Sprinkle with pepper, and the juice of half the lemon.
4. Place liver on a hot serving dish, and decorate each portion with a slice of lemon.

Note: The delicate flavour of calves liver will be lost in this highly seasoned recipe. Use ox, pig's or lamb's liver for this – and the following two recipes. It is more economical.

The Secret of judging the quantity of herbs: Remember dried mixed herbs are roughly twice as strong in flavour as their fresh counterparts. Be careful to use less, until you have worked out the quantity for your particular taste. Do not, however, store dried herbs for too long, or they lose their flavour.

LIVER 'EN MEURETTE'

Preparation and cooking: 30 minutes

For 4
4 thick slices lamb's liver
A little flour (see method)
50g/2oz (*4 Tbsp*) butter or margarine
1 onion, chopped
2 glasses red wine
A sprig of thyme
1 bay leaf
Chopped parsley
250g/8oz (*1¼ cups*) rice
Salt and pepper

17 cm (8-inch diameter) ring mould

1. Put on the rice to cook in plenty of boiling, salted water.
2. Cut the liver into cubes. Roll in seasoned flour. Sauté gently in a frypan or skillet in 30g (generous 1oz, *2 Tbsp*) of the butter or margarine, over moderate heat for 3 minutes. Remove from pan and keep hot.
3. Cook the onion in the frypan or skillet until transparent, add the red wine, thyme, bay leaf, and salt and pepper. Turn up the heat and allow mixture to boil for 5 minutes, stirring to prevent sticking.
4. Mix the rest of the butter into a teaspoon of flour. Add to the pan, little by little, and allow to bubble for a few minutes.
5. Drain rice, rinse in very hot water. Pack into the warmed ring mould and press with the back of a spoon *(a)*. Place serving dish upside-down over mould, invert, and turn out the rice ring *(b)*. Pile the liver in the centre, pour over the sauce *(c)*, and sprinkle with chopped parsley before serving.

Variations: Serve with puréed potatoes, instead of rice. Try cooking the rice in stock instead of water.

The Secret of stopping rice grains from sticking together in cooking: Do not allow to over-cook. Stir frequently during cooking, and when draining with hot water, make holes in the rice with the handle of a wooden spoon to help drain more quickly.

A

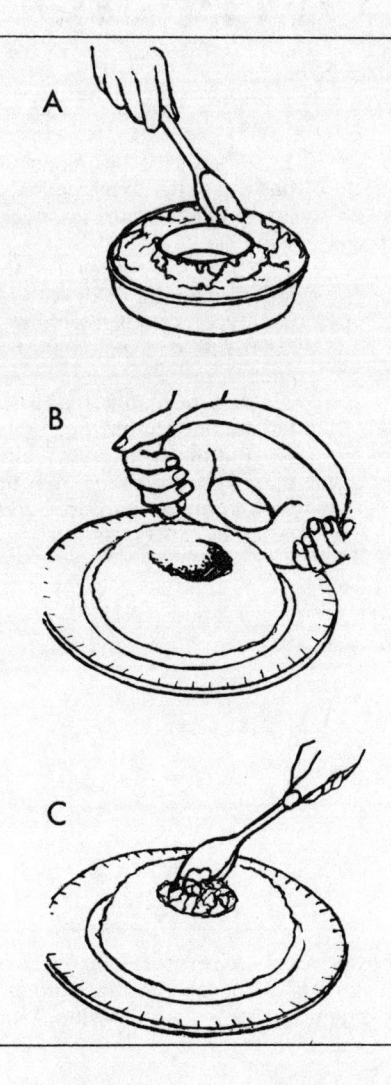

B

C

LIVER AND ONIONS

Preparation and cooking: 20 minutes

For 4
4 slices liver
2 onions
40g/1½oz (*3 Tbsp*) butter or margarine
Parsley
2 tablespoons wine vinegar
A little flour
Salt and pepper

1. Finely slice the onions. Cook very gently with half the butter or margarine, salt and pepper and just enough water to cover them, for about 5 minutes.
2. Chop the parsley. Dip the slices of liver in a little flour and sprinkle with salt and pepper. Cook in a frypan or skillet with the rest of the butter or margarine over moderate heat for 2–3 minutes each side.
3. Add the onions, then the vinegar, and leave to boil for one minute.
4. Put the slices of liver on a hot serving dish, pour over the sauce from the pan and sprinkle with chopped parsley. Serve with plain boiled potatoes or noodles.

The Secret of cooking liver without spattering fat: Make sure that it is well coated in flour beforehand. This absorbs any surface liquid and makes a crust which cooks gently in melted butter, without spattering.

KIDNEYS BAUGÉ

Preparation and cooking: 20 minutes

For 4
2 calves' kidneys
100g/4oz (*1¼ cups*) button mushrooms
1 thick slice cooked ham
50g/2oz (*4 Tbsp*) butter or margarine
100g/4fl.oz (*¼ pint*) thick cream
1 liqueur glass brandy
Salt and pepper
Croûtes to serve (optional, see method)

1. Clean the mushrooms and dice them. Cut the ham into strips. Put half the butter in a frypan or skillet and cook the mushrooms and ham quickly over a high heat. Add salt, pepper and the cream. Leave to bubble for 2 minutes.

2. Meanwhile, skin, de-core and dice the kidneys, being careful to remove any white membranes. Sauté them very quickly in the rest of the butter in a separate pan over a high heat. Add salt, pepper and pour on the brandy. Heat to boiling point, then quickly set the brandy alight. (It should burn with a blue flame.) Dish up kidneys immediately on a hot serving dish with the mushroom sauce poured over. Serve with croûtes of bread (optional).

Croûtes. Slices of stale white bread, cut into rounds or triangles, and fried on both sides in a little hot oil. Drain on absorbent kitchen paper before tucking between each kidney.

The Secret of tender kidneys: Very speedy cooking over high heat – or very slow cooking over low heat. There is an old saying that kidneys are cooked for '2 minutes – or 2 hours'. Otherwise the kidneys will be tough as rubber!

KIDNEYS IN MUSTARD

Preparation and cooking: 15 minutes

For 4
2 veal or 4–6 lambs' kidneys
4 large mushrooms
4 chipolata sausages
40g/1½oz (*3 Tbsp*) butter or margarine
1 glass white wine
1 scant tablespoon strong mustard
Salt and pepper

1. Skin, de-core and dice kidneys, being careful to remove the white membranes. Remove stalks from mushrooms, and sauté heads rapidly, with the chipolatas in a frypan or skillet, with half the butter or margarine. Season with salt and pepper, remove from pan and keep warm.
2. In the same pan, cook the kidneys over a low heat for 3 to 5 minutes, sprinkle with a little salt and remove them from the pan. Keep warm under the grill (broiler) until the sauce is ready.
3. Pour the white wine into the frypan or skillet, and boil up to reduce the quantity of liquid by one-third. Remove from the heat and add the strong mustard, stirring vigorously. Pour over the kidneys and serve accompanied by the chipolatas and mushrooms, and a green vegetable of your choice or puréed potatoes.

The Secret of keeping mustard from curdling while cooking: It must be added to the pan away from the heat source, and mixed in briskly with a sauce whisk or a wooden spoon. Under no circumstances should it be returned to the heat. If it must be re-heated this can only be done in a bain-marie (a roasting tin half-full of water placed in a moderate oven to heat) or a double-boiler.

KIDNEYS IN PORT WINE

Preparation and cooking: 15 minutes

For 4
- 2–3 calves' or pigs' kidneys
- 50g/2oz (*4 Tbsp*) butter or margarine
- Juice of ½ a lemon
- 1 glass port wine
- 1 small jar finely chopped truffles (optional) or 50g/2oz (¾ *cup*) button mushrooms
- ½ teaspoon flour
- Salt and pepper

1. Skin and de-core the kidneys, sauté them briskly in a pan or skillet with half the butter or margarine over a high heat. Season with salt and pepper. After 4–5 minutes, squeeze over a few drops of lemon juice. Remove kidneys from the pan, and keep hot under the grill (broiler).
2. Add the port and the truffles with their liquid (or mushrooms with a little more lemon juice) to the juices in the pan. Allow to boil for about 2 minutes. Meanwhile blend the rest of the butter with the flour. Add this, little by little, to the sauce, beating continuously until the mixture returns to the boil.
3. Return the kidneys to the pan, cover them with the sauce, and serve immediately with creamed potatoes, plain boiled rice or French fries.

The Secret of cooked kidneys which do not taste strong, or strange: Put them in a strainer and dip this into a pan of boiling water with 2 tablespoons vinegar. As soon as the water returns to the boil, drain the kidneys and rinse thoroughly in cold water.

MAITRE D'HOTEL KIDNEYS

Preparation and cooking: 15 minutes
To marinate: 1 hour

For 4
2 calves' or 4–6 lambs' kidneys
30g/1½oz (*3 Tbsp*) butter or margarine
Salt and pepper

The marinade
2–3 pinches mixed dried herbs
4–5 tablespoons cooking oil

The maître d'hôtel butter
20g/¾oz (*scant 2 Tbsp*) butter
Parsley, finely chopped
Juice of ½ a lemon
Salt and pepper

Mustard and cress *or* small cress
Potato crisps

1. Marinate kidneys for 1 hour in the oil with dried herbs.
2. Skin kidneys. Split, but do not cut quite through. Completely remove the white core.
3. Sauté kidneys rapidly in a pan in hot butter or margarine, for 2–3 minutes on each side. Season with salt and pepper as soon as they are cooked. Keep hot under the grill (broiler) to allow them to drain.
4. Make the maître d'hôtel butter. Cut butter into pieces and knead them with the finely chopped parsley, lemon juice, salt and pepper.
5. Arrange a bunch of small cress at each end of a hot serving dish. Place the kidneys in the middle with a piece of herb butter on each. Serve oven-warmed crisps separately.

The Secret of deliciously flavoured kidneys without that bitter taste: Marinating them helps the flavour, but make sure to remove every bit of white core, otherwise the kidneys will taste unpleasantly bitter.

BRAINS MEUNIERE

Preparation and cooking: 1 hour 35 minutes

For 4
2–3 sets calves or 4 sets sheeps' brains
Red or white wine vinegar (see method)
Bouquet garni
1 clove garlic
2 cloves
A little flour
40g/scant 2oz (*4 Tbsp*) butter or margarine
Juice of ½ a lemon
Parsley
Salt and pepper

1. Soak the brains in cold water to cover and 3 tablespoons vinegar for 1 hour. Then, using your fingertips, remove the surrounding membrane and ducts under running water.
2. *The stock.* Put 2 pints water, salt, a bouquet garni, garlic, 6–8 tablespoons vinegar and 2 cloves in a pan. Boil for 5 minutes, then add the brains to the boiling stock. Bring slowly back to the boil and remove from the heat immediately. Leave brains to cool in the stock.
3. Drain very carefully and cut the brains into slices a good centimetre (½ in) thick. Sprinkle the slices with flour and season with salt and pepper.
4. Melt butter or margarine in a large frypan or skillet and add the sliced brains. Brown on one side over gentle heat, then turn with a spatula. Cook slowly for a few more minutes and turn out on to a hot serving dish. Pour the cooking juices and lemon juice over the brains and sprinkle with chopped parsley.

The Secret of brains which do not break up in cooking: They should never be boiled, otherwise they will break up, thus losing their firm, tender texture. They can cook in the stock for up to 12 minutes but *must* be removed before boiling.

SWEETBREADS 'EN COCOTTE'

Preparation and cooking: 1½ hours

For 4
1–2 calves' or lambs' sweetbreads
30g/1½oz (*3 Tbsp*) butter
1 level tablespoon flour
Salt

The stock
1 carrot
2 onions
25g/1oz (*2 Tbsp*) butter
25g/1oz (*2 Tbsp*) flour
1 teaspoon tomato paste
½ bouillon cube
Salt and pepper

1. *The stock*. Peel and dice the carrot and onions. Soften in a frypan or skillet with 25g/1oz (*2 Tbsp*) butter. Add a dust of flour and mix well. Dilute the half bouillon cube in ½ pint boiling water, with the tomato paste and pepper (check for seasoning before adding salt). Pour this over the carrot and onions. Leave to simmer over low heat, without a lid, for about an hour, until thick.
2. *Cooking the sweetbreads*. Plunge them into a pan of cold, salted water. Bring slowly to the boil and leave just on the point of boiling for 5 minutes, the surface of the water should just 'tremble'. Drain and rinse sweetbreads under cold water. Remove any ducts, pipes and skin, then place them between two plates and flatten by placing a kilo (2lb) weight on top. Leave to compress for about an hour.
3. Lightly sprinkle the sweetbreads with flour. Melt the butter in a pan, and lightly brown them over a high heat. Drain. Strain the stock, return it to the rinsed pan and put the sweetbreads to simmer for a further 30 minutes. Serve with small peas and plain boiled potatoes or potato croquettes (*see page 184*).

The Secret of firm sweetbreads: By weighting them down (though not *too* heavily) after boiling briefly in water, they retain their texture when cold and can, if wished, be sliced neatly and easily.

TRIPE ALGER

Preparation and cooking: 4½ hours
In a pressure cooker: 1¼ hours

For 4–6
1½kg/3lb tripe
100g/4oz (½ *cup*) butter or margarine
10 cloves garlic
½ a calf's foot
4 sweet peppers (pimientos)
1 tomato
1 bouquet garni
Cayenne pepper
3–4 pinches caraway seeds
1 pinch cinnamon
Salt

1. Blanch the tripe by placing in a pan of cold water to cover. Bring to the boil and remove pan from heat. Drain and rinse tripe in cold water. Remove the seeds from the pimientos and dice them. Cut the blanched tripe into strips.

2. Heat the butter in a flameproof casserole. Put in the peeled garlic to soften, but not discolour. Add the half calf's foot, peppers, tomato, bouquet garni, salt, cayenne pepper, caraway seeds, cinnamon, ⅔ litre/1 pint (*1¼ pints*) water and the tripe. Cover and cook in a very slow oven (Gas Mark 1, 250 – 275°F, 130°C) for 4½ hours (or 1¼ hours in a pressure cooker on top of the stove). Serve with plain, boiled rice, potatoes, noodles or couscous (Algerian semolina).

A practical dish, since it can be prepared entirely in advance and re-heated.

The Secret of well-cooked tender tripe: It is that it cooks more slowly and steadily in the oven than on the top of the stove. The ideal cooking pot is a cast-iron casserole. If your oven-gloves are thin, wrap the handles of the casserole with kitchen foil. This cools quickly on leaving the oven.

TRIPE AU GRATIN

Preparation and cooking: 1¼ hours

For 4
1kg/2lb cooked tripe
75g/3oz (¾ *cup*) gruyère cheese, grated

The tomato sauce
1 small carrot
1 onion
30g/1½oz (*3 Tbsp*) butter or margarine
1 level tablespoon flour
1 medium-size can (7½oz) tomato purée
1 tomato, peeled and sliced
½ glass white wine
1 teaspoon sugar
Bouquet garni
Salt and pepper

1. *The tomato sauce.* Peel and dice the carrot and onion. Cook in a saucepan with the butter until the onion is transparent. Sprinkle on the flour and stir in well. Add tomato purée, tomato slices, white wine, sugar, bouquet garni and ½ litre/¾ pint (*1 pint*) water. Adjust seasoning, and bring to the boil. Cover and allow to simmer for about 30 minutes.
2. Meanwhile, rinse well and cut the tripe into strips, and place in a gratin dish. Sprinkle over half the grated cheese. When the tomato sauce is cooked, pour this over the cheese and finish with the rest of the cheese. Place in a hot oven (Gas Mark 7–8, 425 – 450°F, 215 – 225°C) for 30 minutes. Serve with plain boiled potatoes.

The Secret of a quick tomato sauce: Use a medium-size can (*1½ cups*) canned Italian tomatoes, as a base. Heat through adding a little flour, dried onion flakes, seasoning and a little sugar and a pinch of mixed herbs to taste. Stir in a little butter and reduce liquid over high heat before adding wine, otherwise sauce will not be thick enough.

MAIN COURSE DISHES: POULTRY AND GAME

Chicken, that most versatile of meats, used to be a luxury dish. Now it is one of the most popular and easily available of birds, and there are many ways of dressing it up. Turkey, too, is now an economical alternative to the Sunday joint, especially on family occasions, and Françoise Bernard has one or two good ideas for using half-turkeys or the packs of turkey joints which are increasingly in the shops. As rabbit is more popular in France than here, we have included some recipes for this, and if you find pigeon, partridge or quail hard to come by, try out the recipes with poussins (baby chickens) instead.

OVEN ROAST CHICKEN

Preparation and cooking: 1¼ hours

For 4
1 large chicken, weighing 1½kg/about 3lb
50g/2oz (*4 Tbsp*) butter or margarine
Salt and pepper

1. Set the oven at Gas Mark 6, 400°F, 200°C ten minutes before cooking.
2. Season the inside of the bird with salt and pepper and drop in half the butter or margarine. Coat the outside with the rest of the butter or margarine and sprinkle with salt and pepper.
3. Place the chicken in a roasting pan and cook in the centre of the oven, allowing about 25 to 30 minutes per lb. After 15 minutes, turn the chicken on to one side then 45 minutes later, turn it on to the other side and finish roasting on its stomach. Serve the chicken, carved or whole, on a large serving dish with game chips or French fries, and garnished with watercress.

SPIT ROAST CHICKEN

Preparation and cooking: 1¼ hours

For 4
1 large chicken, weighing 1½kg/3½lb
50g/2oz *(4 Tbsp)* butter or margarine
Salt and pepper

1. Replace the liver from the giblet sac back into the chicken. Season inside with salt and pepper and add half the butter or margarine. Fix the chicken on to the spit lengthways, making sure that it is evenly balanced all the way round the skewer, to ensure even roasting.
2. Fix the spit in the middle of the rôtisserie or oven and set turning. When the chicken has cooked for about an hour and is thoroughly browned, it should be ready to eat.

The Secrets of succulent roast chicken: To give the chicken extra flavour, put a few sprigs of thyme, rosemary or a bunch of tarragon inside.

To test whether the chicken is cooked, lift it up with the point of a fork and tip it neck downwards over the serving dish. The juice which pours out through the neck should be colourless. If even the last few drops are a little pink, cook it a little longer.

Once cooked, the chicken can be left for a moment or two in a low oven. It will taste even better if left for at least 10 minutes in a switched-off oven.

Roast chicken which is to be eaten cold should be wrapped and sealed in kitchen foil and not carved until it is just about to be eaten.

🔑 *In the oven*:
It is better to stand the chicken on a small wire-mesh tray, such as that used for grilling (broiling), in the roasting tin. If it is placed directly on the bottom of the tin, it tends to overcook in its own juice.

Baste regularly throughout roasting.

Never add water to the roasting tin, a chicken always produces enough juice to baste itself.

For the gravy: After removing the chicken from the roasting pan, add a little water and boil this up, stirring and scraping sides with a wooden spoon to remove all the tiny pieces of meat stuck to the bottom of the pan.

🔑 *On the spit*:
It is better to put all the butter inside the chicken, rather than to coat the outside. Baste regularly if the spit is in an oven and even more often if it is on a rôtisserie or barbecue. If the spit does not turn automatically, give it a quarter turn every 10 minutes. If the spit is in an oven, remember to cook with the door ajar.

STUFFINGS FOR CHICKEN

A stuffed roast chicken looks better and is tastier than one which has simply been roasted. Here are five good recipes for stuffing to which you can add your personal touch. Each should fill a 1½kg/3lb bird.

ENGLISH STUFFING

100g/4oz rye bread
2 onions, chopped
50g/2oz (*4 Tbsp*) butter or margarine
50g/2oz (*4 Tbsp*) beef marrow
2 chicken livers, chopped
Nutmeg
Salt and pepper

Finely crumble the bread (there should be about a cupful). Put in a frypan or skillet with the chopped onions and the butter or margarine. Allow to cook over a very low heat. Immerse the marrow in water which is just coming to the boil and poach for 5 minutes off the heat. Mix together the cooked bread and onion mixture, marrow, chopped livers, salt, pepper and two pinches of ground nutmeg.

TARRAGON STUFFING

200g/8oz mushrooms
125g/4–5oz bacon
1 chicken liver
1 shallot
1 clove garlic
Fresh or dried tarragon
Salt and pepper

Finely chop all the ingredients and mix together, including the leaves from several sprigs of tarragon (or 2 pinches dried tarragon). Season generously with salt and pepper.

LIVER STUFFING

3 poultry livers, chopped
100g/4oz white bread
1 glass milk
250g/10oz mushrooms
25g/1oz (*2 Tbsp*) butter
1 tablespoon brandy
Salt and pepper
1 egg, beaten

Soak the bread in warm milk in a bowl. Clean and chop the mushrooms and sauté them, with the chopped livers, in a frypan or skillet with the butter or margarine and salt and pepper, for 5 minutes. Add the brandy. Leave on a high heat for a few minutes then mix in the soaked bread, and bind with beaten egg.

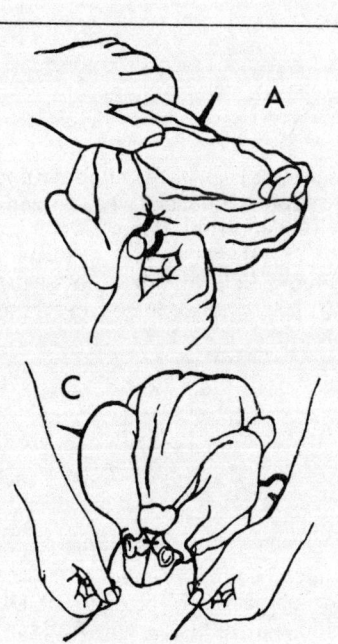

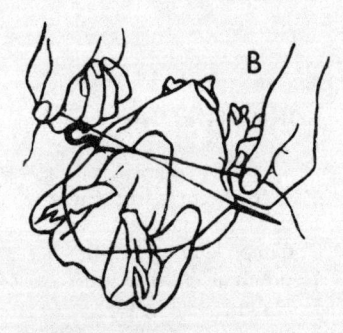

Trussing Chicken with a Skewer

(a) Insert skewer below thighs.

(b) Cross string over back of bird.

(c) Loop string round the drumsticks.

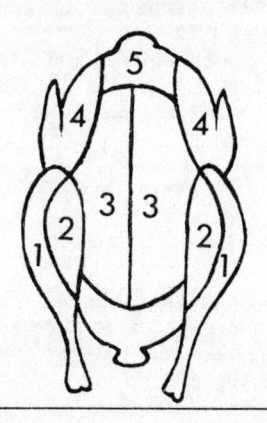

Jointing
1. Drumsticks
2. Thighs
3. Breast
4. Wings
5. Carcass for stock

CORN STUFFING

1 large can sweetcorn (at least 198g or 7oz)
50g/2oz ($\frac{1}{4}$ cup) forcemeat (sausagemeat)
1 chicken liver
10 green olives, stoned
1 red pepper, chopped
A few lettuce leaves, chopped
30g/1$\frac{1}{2}$oz (*3 Tbsp*) butter or margarine
1 egg, beaten
Salt and pepper

Place the forcemeat, liver, olives, chopped pepper and several chopped lettuce leaves in a pan and cook over low heat in the butter or margarine. Season with salt and pepper. After a few minutes add the sweetcorn. Cook just long enough to heat corn through, then remove pan from heat, and stir in the beaten egg.

RICH STUFFING

2 onions, chopped
30g/1$\frac{1}{2}$oz (*3 Tbsp*) butter or margarine
100g/4oz pork
100g/4oz shoulder or pie veal
1 chicken liver and gizzard
1 egg, beaten
Nutmeg
Fresh or dried thyme
$\frac{1}{2}$ bay leaf
Salt and pepper

Cook the chopped onions for about 12 minutes in the butter or margarine. Mince (grind) all the meats and bind with the beaten egg. Add salt and pepper, a pinch of ground nutmeg, a few leaves of fresh thyme (or a pinch of dried thyme), a crushed half bay leaf. Finally, mix in the cooked onions.

The stuffings should be packed inside the chicken. To ensure that they do not seep out while cooking, either sew up the neck well or pull the excess skin over it and draw up the feet before binding them to this skin with a strong twine, thus sealing the opening.

COLD CHICKEN IN ASPIC

Preparation: ¾ hour
Leave to cool: 1 hour

For 4
1 roast chicken, (weighing 1½kg/about 3lb)
½ litre/1 pint aspic jelly, made up according to the instructions on the packet
1 tablespoon port wine

The garnish
Fresh tarragon
4 tomatoes, quartered
Green salad

1. Cut up the cold chicken and put the pieces on a wire tray, over a serving dish.
2. Prepare the jelly, flavouring it with the port. When it cools to the consistency of oil, spoon a little over the chicken. When well-coated, leave in a cool place to set.
3. *To garnish.* Dip the tarragon leaves in the liquid aspic and arrange them on the breast of the chicken. Leave to set for a few more minutes.
4. Pour the rest of the aspic over the bottom of the serving dish. Leave this to cool and set.
5. Arrange the chicken pieces on the bed of jelly. Surround the chicken with peeled, quartered tomatoes and green salad. Artichoke hearts, potato crisps, asparagus tips, eggs stuffed with caviare or lumpfish roe (poor man's caviare) also make good accompaniments.

The Secret of well-flavoured aspic: Replace 1–2 tablespoons of water used in making the aspic with port wine or dry sherry. This gives the aspic a deliciously savoury taste.

FOWL-IN-THE-POT

Preparation and cooking: 3½ hours
In a pressure cooker: 1½ hours

For 4 or 6
1 boiling fowl (stewing chicken), weighing 1½ – 1¾kg/3½– 4lb
2 veal bones
1 onion
2 cloves
1 stick of celery, diced
Bouquet garni
4 carrots, sliced
4 turnips, sliced
6 leeks, sliced
Salt and pepper
8–12 slices crisp fried bread

1. Put the veal bones, chicken giblets, the onion stuffed with the cloves, celery, bouquet garni, salt and pepper in a large saucepan of cold water to cover. Bring to the boil and skim well.
2. Immerse the chicken in the boiling stock and simmer very slowly for 2½–3 hours (in a pressure cooker: about 1 hour). Add the carrots, turnips and leeks halfway through cooking.
3. Skim the stock well and serve as a gravy with triangles of crisp fried bread. The chicken should be jointed and served in a deep dish, surrounded by the cooked vegetables, accompanied by rock salt and pickled gherkins.

If serving this dish with boiled rice, it can be accompanied by a white sauce made with the skimmed chicken stock.

The Secrets of fowl-in-the-pot: Use an elderly boiling fowl to ensure that the meat will not break up during the long cooking.
Do not use too much water in the cooking.
Thoroughly skim all the grease off the surface of the stock.
Keep the chicken white by rubbing it all over with lemon before putting it in the stock.
Ensure that the stock has a nice golden colour by thoroughly browning a large onion (without using butter or fat) and adding it to the stock at the start of the cooking.

COQ AU VIN

Preparation and cooking: 2½ hours
In a pressure cooker: ¾ hour
To marinate: overnight

For 6–8
1 large chicken, weighing 1½–1¾kg/3½b, cut into joints
40g/1½oz (*3 Tbsp*) butter or margarine
100g/4oz belly of pork
1 tablespoon flour
1 liqueur glass brandy
1 tablespoon tomato paste
125g/5oz streaky bacon
250g/9oz mushrooms
Parsley
Salt and pepper

The marinade
1 bottle Chambertin (rich red Burgundy)
2 tablespoons oil
1 onion, chopped
2 shallots, chopped
1 small carrot, chopped
3 cloves garlic
1 bouquet garni
1 clove
3 peppercorns

1. The day before cooking, put the chicken joints and the marinade ingredients in a dish just big enough for the marinade to cover chicken.
2. On the day of cooking, drain the meat and the spices separately, and reserve the liquid in which they have been marinated.
3. Cut up the belly of pork and heat it in a flameproof casserole with the butter or margarine. Brown the pieces of chicken all over, except the liver. Now add the spices from the marinade and sprinkle with the flour. Mix the ingredients together gently, pour on the brandy, bring it to the boil, then set alight. When the flames have subsided, add the marinade liquid, one glass of water, the tomato paste, salt and pepper. Cover and simmer for 1½–2 hours.
4. Dice the bacon and fry it over a low heat, then sauté the sliced mushrooms in the fat.
5. Place the chicken pieces on a warm serving dish with the mushrooms and diced bacon. If the sauce is not thick enough, reduce it by rapid boiling over a high heat. Mince (grind) the chicken liver and stir it into the sauce. Remove from the heat immediately and pour the sauce over the chicken. Sprinkle with parsley before serving with plain boiled potatoes, or tagliatelli.

The Secret of a velouté sauce for coq au vin: the raw minced liver, mixed into the sauce at the end of the cooking, brings it to just the right consistency. Do not let it boil after adding this or the sauce will curdle.

CHICKEN SAUTÉ VALLEE D'AUGE

Preparation and cooking: 1¼ hours
In a pressure cooker: 20–25 minutes

For 4
1 jointed chicken, weighing 1½ – 1¾kg/3 – 3½lb
30g/1½oz (*3 Tbsp*) butter or margarine
1 liqueur glass Calvados
2 egg yolks
225g/8fl oz (1 cup) thick cream
Salt and pepper

1. Slightly sauté the chicken joints in a flameproof casserole in butter or margarine but do not allow to brown. Add the salt and pepper, cover and leave to simmer over a low heat in its own juices for about 1 hour (in a pressure cooker: 20 to 25 minutes).
2. Pour the Calvados over the cooked chicken. Bring to the boil and set alight immediately. When the flames subside, take out the chicken and place it on a hot serving dish.
3. Mix the egg yolks with the fresh cream and add them to the cooking juices in the pan, still on the stove, but without allowing it to boil. Stir continuously with a wooden spoon. Pour a little of this sauce over the chicken and the rest into a hot sauceboat.
   Serve with plain boiled rice or potatoes.

The Secret of a smooth, thick cream sauce: The cooking juices must be very thoroughly skimmed before the cream and egg yolks are added, otherwise the mixture will become too greasy and, instead of thickening, it will curdle. Do not allow to boil after adding the egg and cream mixture.

CHICKEN MARTINIQUE

Preparation and cooking: 1 hour

For 4
1 jointed chicken, weighing 1kg/about 2½ lbs
30g/1½oz (*3 Tbsp*) butter or margarine
1 carrot, chopped
2 onions, chopped
½ teaspoon curry powder
Pinch saffron
1 clove of garlic
Bouquet garni
150g/6oz (*scant cup*) rice
Salt and pepper

1. Quickly brown the chicken joints in butter or margarine in a large flameproof casserole. Halfway through, add the chopped carrots and onions so that they can also brown.
2. Add the curry powder, saffron, crushed garlic, bouquet garni, salt, pepper and ½ litre/1 pint (*1¼ pints*) of water. Bring to the boil and leave to simmer, covered, for twenty minutes.
3. Wash the rice in running water, add it to the casserole and simmer dish for a further 17–20 minutes, adding a little more water if necessary.

The Secret of chicken Martinique: Browning the carrots and onions before adding water, gives the resulting stock a richer flavour.

CHICKEN PROVENÇAL

Preparation and cooking: 1 hour

For 4
1 jointed chicken, weighing 1½kg/3lb
30g/1½oz (*3 Tbsp*) butter or margarine
1 tablespoon flour
3 tomatoes
1 clove garlic
Fresh or dried basil
½ bottle dry white wine
Bouquet garni
125g/6oz (*2 cups*) mushrooms
20 stoned black olives
2 tablespoons chopped parsley
Salt and pepper

1. Brown the chicken joints all over in a flameproof casserole, in the butter or margarine. Sprinkle the flour over and stir to mix. Add the tomatoes, chopped, garlic, a pinch or two of dried basil (or 4–5 leaves of fresh), the wine, ¼ litre/½ pint (*1¼ pints*) water and the bouquet garni. Season with salt and pepper. Half cover the pan and leave to simmer for 30 minutes.
2. Wash the mushrooms and slice them. Add to the casserole with the olives. Cook for a further 15 minutes. Remove the bouquet garni. Place the chicken pieces in a hot serving dish and pour the sauce over. Sprinkle with chopped parsley.

The Secret of a well-browned chicken: Place the pieces to brown on the skin side first, then turn over. To save time, you can use ready-bought chicken pieces instead of a whole chicken.

TURKEY WITH MUSHROOM STUFFING

Preparation and cooking: 3 hours
Standing time: ½ hour

For 10
1 turkey, weighing 4kg/9–10lb
50g/2oz (*4 Tbsp*) butter or margarine
2 tablespoons port wine
Salt and pepper

The stuffing
2 cans mushrooms, 198g/7oz each, or 400g/1lb fresh mushrooms
½ glass warm milk
50g/2oz bread
300g/11oz pork forcemeat (sausagemeat)
½ glass port wine
1 egg, beaten
Turkey liver, diced
Salt and pepper

1. *The stuffing*. Wash and drain the mushrooms, dice the tops and finely chop the stalks. Pour the warm milk over the bread in a mixing bowl. Add the mushrooms, the pork, port wine, egg, the diced turkey liver, salt and pepper. Mash together and stuff the turkey without packing the mixture too firmly. Truss and close the openings.
2. Put the turkey on its side in a large roasting pan and coat with the butter or margarine. Sprinkle with salt and pepper. Cook in the oven (Gas Mark 5–6, 375 – 400°F, 190 – 200°C) for 1 hour on each side, and finally, 30 minutes on its back, basting frequently.
3. When the turkey is cooked, switch off the oven and leave the bird in it for half-an-hour, then remove the turkey and put on a hot serving dish. Pour the cooking juices into a pan, bring to the boil and skim. Allow to boil a little longer to thicken the gravy. Add the port and pour the gravy immediately into a sauceboat to serve with the turkey carved in slices.

: *Touch the fleshy part of the thigh, which should feel very supple. Move the drumstick backwards and forwards. It should move freely, and offer no resistance.*

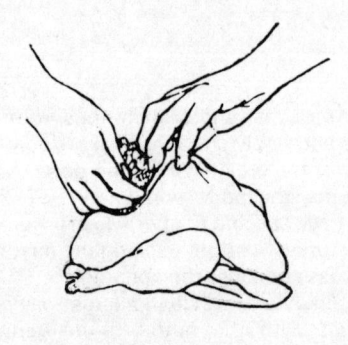

Stuffing and Trussing Turkey
After skewering the skin of the neck, stuff the bird through the parson's nose end. Don't over-fill the cavity as the stuffing will expand during cooking.

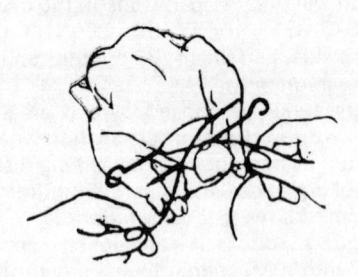

Insert two skewers across the opening and wind string across as shown. Then draw the string tightly round the end of the legs before fastening off.

STUFFINGS FOR ROAST TURKEY OR GOOSE

To fill a 4 kilo/8–10lb bird

PÉRIGOURDINE

250g/10oz turkey or poultry liver
2 shallots, chopped
25g/1oz (*2 Tbsp*) butter or margarine
4 small sweet bread rolls (brioches)
¾ glass milk
1 198g/7oz can mushrooms

1. Dice the poultry livers and sauté them with the chopped shallots in the butter or margarine. Put the rolls to soak in the warm milk.
2. Drain then wash the mushrooms, chop the stalks and dice the heads. Mix together with the soaked brioches and the fried liver and shallots.

POULTRY LIVER STUFFING

500g/1lb poultry livers, diced
200g/7oz thin slices streaky (fat) bacon
2 onions, chopped
200g/8oz fresh white bread
50g/2oz (*4 Tbsp*) butter or margarine
Salt and pepper

1. Fry the bacon in a pan and add the chopped onions and diced livers. Simmer for 10 minutes.
2. Pour this into a large bowl containing the crumbled bread, melted butter or margarine and season with salt and pepper. Mash the lot together and leave to cool.

SAUSAGE AND CELERY STUFFING

800/2lb (4 cups) sausage-meat (forcemeat)
4 sticks celery
2 onions
Parsley
25g/1oz (*2 Tbsp*) butter or margarine
1 egg, beaten
Salt and pepper

Finely chop the celery, onions and parsley. Mix together and bind with the melted butter. Mix together and bind with the melted butter, beaten egg and salt and pepper. Add the forcemeat and mix thoroughly.

To serve stuffing attractively: When the bird is carved, the stuffing may be removed in one piece and cut into slices to serve with the turkey or goose.

SPECIAL CHESTNUT STUFFING

1 can chestnuts, 538g/1lb 3oz
100g/4oz veal
100g/4oz pork
The poultry liver (turkey or goose)
100g/4oz fresh streaky (fat) bacon
1 or 2 shallots, or small onions
1 egg, beaten
1 cup white breadcrumbs
1 liqueur glass brandy
Salt and pepper

Mince the veal, pork, poultry liver and diced bacon together with the peeled shallots. In another bowl, mix the egg with the breadcrumbs, salt, pepper, brandy and the chestnuts, mashed with a fork. Add the minced meats and shallots and mix all the ingredients together well.

Note: Be careful when buying canned chestnut purée instead of whole chestnuts. Cans of purée are often sweetened for use in desserts.

NUT STUFFING

60g/3oz shelled walnuts
30g/1½oz cashew nuts
30g/1½oz Brazil nuts
2 onions
50g/2oz (*4 Tbsp*) butter or margarine
200g/8oz mushrooms
250g/8oz fresh white breadcrumbs
2 eggs, beaten
1 tablespoon chopped parsley
Salt and pepper

1. Chop the onions and cook them gently for 5 minutes in the butter or margarine.
2. Finely chop the mushrooms, add them to the onion and cook, covered, for a further 5 minutes.
3. Crush the nuts well (with a rolling pin or in a blender) and mix them with the chopped parsley, breadcrumbs, beaten eggs, and the onion and mushroom mixture. Season with salt and pepper (if necessary, this can be moistened with a little poultry stock).

TURKEY BROCHETTES

Preparation and cooking: 1¼ hours
To marinate: 1 hour

For 4
700g/1½lb raw turkey meat
2–3 slices lean bacon
Juice of 1 lemon
2–3 tablespoons oil
Fresh or dried thyme
Salt and pepper

4 long barbecue skewers

1. One hour before cooking, cut the turkey meat into cubes. Mix with the lemon juice, thyme, salt, pepper and oil. When ready to cook, cut the bacon into strips, thread on to the skewers alternately with pieces of turkey meat. Brush each brochette with a little oil. Wrap in kitchen foil and leave for an hour in a cool place.
2. Remove the foil and cook the brochettes under the grill (broiler) for 15 minutes, turning several times, and brushing with a little extra oil if necessary. Keep warm for 10 minutes before serving.

Serve with canned sweetcorn, heated through in a little butter, peas or green beans, or wrap again in foil and eat cold, for a picnic.

The Secret of perfect turkey brochettes: Marinating the rather dry meat tenderizes and softens it. You can also cut bacon into strips and wrap a strip round each piece of turkey meat before cooking.

BRAISED TURKEY OR GOOSE

Preparation and cooking: 1½ hours
In a pressure cooker: 20 minutes

For 4
1¼kg/3lb turkey or goose meat
50g/2oz (*4 Tbsp*) butter or margarine
1 carrot
1 onion
1 liqueur glass brandy
Bouquet garni
Salt and pepper

1. Brown the pieces of meat all over in a frypan or skillet with half the butter, over a fairly high heat.
2. Dice the carrot and onion and slightly brown them in a flameproof casserole in the rest of the butter or margarine. Add the browned meat and the brandy. Bring to the boil and set alight. When the flames have subsided, add two glasses of water, season with salt and pepper, add the bouquet garni and simmer – closely covered – for about 1 hour (in a pressure cooker: 20 minutes). Serve with macaroni with the cooking juices poured over the pasta.

The Secret of flaming brandy successfully: Make sure that the brandy is heated or it will not catch alight. This process burns off excess fat, the alcohol evaporates, and the juices left add flavour to the sauce.

CURRIED TURKEY OR GOOSE

Preparation and cooking: 1½ hours
In a pressure cooker: 25 minutes

For 4
1½kg/3lb turkey/goose meat
1 carrot
1 onion
1 leek
1 clove garlic
Bouquet garni
Salt and pepper

The pilaff
200g/8oz (*1¼ cups*) rice
1 onion
30g/1½oz (*3 Tbsp*) butter or margarine
Salt and pepper

The curry sauce
2 onions
30g/1½oz (*3 Tbsp*) butter or margarine
1 tablespoon flour
1–2 teaspoons curry powder (see *Secret*)
½ litre/approx. 1¼ pints (*1¼ pints*) stock
100g/4oz thick cream

1. Immerse the poultry pieces in boiling water for 3 minutes and then drain. Rinse them in cold water immediately, then put them back in the casserole with 1¼ litres/generous 2 pints (2½ *pints*) of water, the peeled carrot, onion, cleaned leek, garlic, bouquet garni, salt and pepper. Simmer gently for about an hour (in a pressure cooker: 25 minutes).

2. *The pilaff.* Chop and brown the onion in the butter or margarine. Add the rice. Stir it in and immediately add twice as much water. Season with salt and pepper. Cover and leave to cook on a very low heat for 15–17 minutes.

3. *The curry sauce.* Chop the onions and sauté them in a small flameproof casserole with the butter or margarine. Shake the flour over them and a teaspoon of curry powder.

Mix together well and moisten with ½ litre/1 pint (*1¼ pints*) of the poultry stock. Stir well until thick, then leave to simmer on a very low heat for 10 minutes. Finally add the cream. Pack the rice into a ring mould and turn it out on to a hot plate. Cut the turkey meat into strips and arrange in the centre of the rice. Pour over the curry sauce and serve.

The Secret of good curry sauce: It depends on your taste. Add more, or less, curry powder as you wish. You can also serve plain boiled rice, without the onion.

GOOSE STUFFED WITH CHESTNUTS

Preparation and cooking: 3 hours

For 8–10
1 large goose
75g/3oz (*6 Tbsp*) butter or margarine
Salt and pepper
Watercress to garnish

The stuffing
100g/4oz ($\frac{1}{2}$ *cup*) collar (lean) bacon
100g/4oz ($\frac{1}{2}$ *cup*) fresh streaky (fat) bacon
100g/4oz ($\frac{1}{2}$ *cup*) veal
The goose liver
2 shallots
1 538g/1lb 3oz can chestnuts
Salt and pepper

1. *Making the stuffing.* Chop up the two sorts of bacon, the veal, liver and shallots. Mash the chestnuts and mix into the other ingredients. Season with salt and pepper and stuff the goose with the mixture. Sew up and truss the goose after stuffing.
2. Coat the thighs with butter or margarine and season with salt and pepper. Put in a hot oven (Gas Mark 7–8, 425–450°F, 220–230°C) for about 30 minutes, then reduce the heat (Gas Mark 6, 400°F, 200°C) for a further 2 hours. Baste regularly throughout the cooking.
3. Serve the goose on a large dish garnished with watercress. Serve the cooking gravy separately as a sauce – but be sure to skim the grease off first.

Note: If a goose or a turkey starts to brown too much or too quickly, place a small piece of aluminium foil over the affected area.

The Secret of canned chestnuts which do not have too watery a taste: Soak them for about 15 minutes in a concentrated poultry stock, made for example, from goose giblets, or 1–2 bouillon cubes. This is long enough to flavour them and, when mashed with a fork, a little more of the same stock can be added to the chestnuts.

ROAST DUCK

Preparation and cooking: 1¼ hours

For 4
1 duckling, 1½kg/3–4lb in weight
30g/1½oz (*3 Tbsp*) butter or margarine
Salt and pepper

1. Lightly brown the duck in the butter in a large flameproof casserole. When it is well browned all over, season. Put the casserole dish, uncovered, into a hot oven (Gas Mark 7, 425°F, 220°C) and leave to cook for 40–45 minutes, basting often. Leave in the oven for 10 minutes, with the heat turned off, before carving.
2. Carve the duck. Arrange the pieces on a hot serving dish. Dilute the cooking juices in the casserole with 2–3 tablespoons boiling water. Reheat, scraping the base and sides of the casserole well with a wooden spoon. Boil up for a few seconds. Skim off any fat, if necessary, and pour into a warm sauceboat. Serve with glazed, or boiled, turnips.

Note: If you like your duck less well done and pink inside, adjust the cooking time.

The Secret of juicy, not too fatty roast duck: As soon as the fat starts to run from the roasting duck, remove it. Do this from time to time during cooking – after basting. Contrary to what you might expect, a fatty duck which cooks in its own fat dries out! (The same thing happens to pork chops.)

DUCK WITH ORANGE

Preparation and cooking: 2 hours

For 4
1 duck, 2kg/4lb in weight
30g/1½oz (*3 Tbsp*) butter or margarine
3 oranges
1 liqueur glass Curaçao
Juice of ½ lemon
Parsley
Salt and pepper

The basic sauce
The giblets
25g/1oz (*2 Tbsp*) butter or margarine
1 onion, chopped
2 glasses dry white wine
1 carrot, diced
Bouquet garni
Salt and pepper

1. An hour beforehand, prepare the sauce. Lightly fry the giblets with 1 chopped onion, in the butter or margarine. Add 2 glasses of white wine, 2 glasses water, 1 diced carrot, the bouquet garni and salt and pepper. Allow to simmer, without a lid, for almost an hour.
2. In a large flameproof casserole, lightly brown the whole duck in the butter over a high heat. Season and pour the strained sauce over it. Leave to simmer for 50 minutes.
3. Peel one orange so thinly that only the yellow zest (rind) is removed. Snip this into tiny pieces (bâtons). Put these into a pan of cold water, bring to the boil, drain and leave to soak in the Curaçao. Peel this and the other two oranges, removing the pith this time, and cut flesh into rounds.
4. Five minutes before the duck is cooked, add the orange rounds to the casserole with the lemon juice, orange zest (rind) and the Curaçao in which it has been soaked.
5. Arrange the duck on a large hot serving dish. Boil up the sauce for a few minutes to reduce it a little, then pour over the duck. Serve sprinkled with chopped parsley, and the slices of orange arranged around the plate, or on the duck itself. Plain boiled potatoes or rice go best with this rich dish.

The Secret of peeling orange zest: Use a potato peeler if your skill with the knife is not up to much.

NORMANDY DUCK

Preparation and cooking: 1 hour

For 4
1 duck, 1½kg/3–4lb in weight
40g/2oz (*4 Tbsp*) butter or margarine
2 liqueur glasses Calvados
1 glass of dry white wine
4 apples
4 or 5 tablespoons thick cream
Sprigs of fresh tarragon, or dried tarragon
Salt and pepper

1. Remove the tarragon leaves from the sprigs. Slide the stalks into the duck (or sprinkle dried herbs inside). Season with salt and pepper. Brown the duck all over in a flameproof casserole in half the butter. Pour on the Calvados, warm, and set alight. Then cover and leave to simmer on a medium heat for 45 minutes. Turn duck two or three times while cooking. If the cooking juice evaporates too fast, add a tablespoonful or two of water.
2. When the duck is cooked, remove and place on a serving dish and keep warm. Add the glass of white wine to the cooking juices. Boil up, uncovered, and reduce liquid to one half in quantity.
3. Peel and cut the apples into thick slices, brown quickly in a frypan or skillet in the remaining butter. Place around the duck.
4. Add the cream and chopped tarragon leaves (or a pinch of dried tarragon) to the cooking juices and boil for a few seconds, stirring with a wooden spoon. Pour into a sauceboat and serve with the duck.

The Secret of a full-flavoured sauce: The cooking juices must be well reduced to concentrate the flavour and thicken the sauce. Stir with a wooden spoon after adding the cream to prevent sticking.

PARTRIDGE ON CANAPÉS

Preparation and cooking: 30 minutes

For 4
2 large partridges
50g/2oz (*4 Tbsp*) butter or margarine
2 vine leaves
2 thin slices of streaky (fat) bacon
2 slices of white bread
A little extra butter, if necessary
Thyme leaves
Salt and pepper

1. Take out the livers and put them on one side. Coat the partridges with half the butter and season them. Place a vine leaf on the stomach of each bird, wrap a slice of bacon round each and tie this on with trussing string. Roast in a hot oven (Gas Mark 6–7, 400–425°F, 200–220°C) for 20 minutes, basting regularly.
2. Lightly fry the bread until crisp in a frypan or skillet in the rest of the butter or margarine. Dice the livers and fry them quickly in a little extra butter. Add salt, pepper, thyme leaves and crush with a fork before spreading on to the bread. Put these canapés on a dish.
3. Take the streaky bacon and vine leaves off the partridges, putting the leaves on one side. Return the partridges to the oven for a further 5 minutes to brown all over. Decorate each bird with a vine leaf and serve on the canapés. Skim the cooking gravy and serve separately in a sauceboat.

Note: If the partridges are only medium-sized, pick 4, and use 4 vine leaves, 4 slices of bacon and 4 slices of bread for the canapés. If vine leaves are hard to obtain, garnish the finished dish with watercress instead.

The Secret of easily skimming the gravy made from cooking game: Bring it to the boil. The boiling forces the grease and fat to stick against the sides of the pan and forms a thick layer which is very easy to remove with a spoon or palette knife.

QUAIL WITH GRAPES

Preparation and cooking: 30 minutes

For 4
4 quail, barded and trussed (see method)
4 slices bacon
250g/8oz white grapes
70g/3oz ($\frac{1}{3}$ *cup)* butter or margarine
The livers from the birds
1 small wineglass brandy
Salt and pepper

The garnish
8 slices bread
50g/2oz (*4 Tbsp)* butter

1. Wrap a slice of bacon round each bird to cover the breast and tie in position, like a parcel, with trussing string. Remove crusts from bread. In a frypan or skillet, gently fry the slices of bread in the butter. Peel the grapes.
2. Quickly brown the quails in a flameproof serving dish in 30g/1$\frac{1}{2}$oz (*3 Pbsp*) butter or margarine. Then cover pan and, turning down the heat, allow them to cook gently for 10 minutes.
3. Sauté the livers quickly in 20g/1oz (*2 Tbsp)* butter and pour over half the brandy. Warm, set alight and when the flames have subsided, crush the livers with a fork. Beat in the rest of the butter, and season with salt and pepper. Spread this over the slices of bread, transfer to a serving dish and keep warm.
4. Remove trussing strings and bacon from birds. Skim the fat from the sauce. Place the birds in the casserole, pour over the rest of the cognac. Set alight and add the grapes. Cover casserole and leave to cook for 2 minutes over gentle heat. Place the birds on the croûtes of bread, pour over the cooking juices and serve, with the grapes.

Note: This recipe is also suitable for partridge, but adjust cooking time to 25–30 minutes. The same applies, for the USA, to Cornish hens.

The Secret of peeling grapes successfully: Use the point of a very sharp knife to score the skin. They should then peel easily. And to de-seed them, pull a curly paper clip into an 's' shape, push into the grape from the top twist – and pull up to remove the pips. No problem.

PIGEONS GRAND-MERE

Preparation and cooking: 1 hour
In a pressure cooker: 15 minutes

For 4
2 large pigeons
85g/3½oz (*scant ½ cup*) butter or margarine
750g/1¾lb potatoes
250g/10oz button (pickling) onions
250g/10oz button mushrooms
Chopped parsley
Salt and pepper

1. Peel the potatoes and onions. Dice and immerse them for 5 minutes in boiling water, then drain.
2. Burn off any remaining pigeon feathers. Season the insides with salt and pepper.
3. Put the pigeons in a large flameproof casserole. Brown them all over in half the butter or margarine. Remove them and in their place quickly brown the onions and potatoes.
4. When the vegetables are golden, replace the pigeons and add a pinch of salt and pepper. Cover the casserole and cook for 45 minutes over medium heat (in a pressure cooker: 15 minutes).
5. Wash the mushrooms and halve them. Sauté them in a frypan or skillet in the rest of the butter. Season them and add to the casserole. Sprinkle with chopped parsley and serve.

Note: A few strips of streaky bacon sautéed or quickly blanched in boiling water can be added to the casserole halfway through cooking. In the USA, this recipe is also suitable for cooking Cornish hens.

The Secret of carving pigeons: There is no need. Simply split them down the middle, lengthways, with a sharp knife.

STUFFED PIGEONS TOULOUSE

Preparation and cooking: 50 minutes

For 4
2 large pigeons
100g/4oz (½ *cup*) bacon, chopped
100g/4oz (½ *cup*) veal, minced (ground)
1 teaspoon mixed herbs
1 egg yolk
30g/1½oz (*3 Tbsp*) butter or margarine
Salt and pepper

1. *The stuffing.* Finely chop the pigeon livers and mix with the bacon and minced veal; add the mixed herbs and bind with the egg yolk. Season with salt and pepper.
2. Stuff the pigeons and truss. Brown them all over in a flameproof casserole with a little butter or margarine. Then put in a hot oven (Gas Mark 6–7, 400 – 425°F, 200 – 220°C) for 40 to 50 minutes. Halfway through cooking add salt and pepper to stop the birds from drying out.

Note: Cornish hens, in the USA, can be cooked in this way.

The Secret of making a tough old pigeon as tender as a young bird: Be sure to cook it in the oven, with the casserole lid *on*. The steam from cooking is retained and makes the meat tender, without making it soggy. When using an old bird allow 5 or 10 minutes extra for cooking.

RABBIT WITH SHALLOTS

Preparation and cooking: ¾ hour
In a pressure cooker: 10 minutes

For 4
1 rabbit, cut in joints
4 tablespoons oil
6 shallots
1 level tablespoon flour
1 liqueur glass dry white wine
Bouquet garni
Parsley
Salt and pepper

1. Brown the rabbit pieces over high heat in the oil.
2. Chop the shallots. Add them to the rabbit with the flour and stir until mixed well. Then add the wine, salt, pepper and the bouquet garni. Leave to simmer, tightly covered, over a very gentle heat for 25 minutes (in a pressure cooker: 8 minutes).
3. Chop the parsley, add to the rabbit and cook for a further 5 minutes.

The Secret of Rabbit with Shallots: You don't *have* to use shallots which can be difficult to obtain as well as expensive. The taste won't be quite the same, but you can use small onions instead.

FLEMISH RABBIT

Preparation and cooking: 1 hour
Marinate overnight

For 4
1 rabbit, cut in joints
30g/1½oz (*3 Tbsp*) butter or margarine
500g/1lb (*3 cups*) prunes
2 tablespoons redcurrant jelly

The marinade
2 carrots, chopped
3 onions, chopped
1 stick celery, chopped
2 cloves, garlic, crushed
1 shallot, chopped
2 cloves
Thyme
Bay leaf
¼ litre/½ pint (*1¼ cups*) vinegar
¼ litre/½ pint (*1¼ cups*) dry white wine
2 tablespoons oil
Salt and pepper

1. *The marinade.* Put the rabbit joints to marinate the night before in a bowl containing all the marinade ingredients. Cover with the vinegar and white wine.
2. The next day, drain the rabbit well, reserving the marinade. Brown on all sides in the butter or margarine. Boil up the marinade for 5 minutes, then strain and pour over the rabbit. Leave to simmer for 30–45 minutes, adding the prunes halfway through the cooking time.
3. Arrange the rabbit on a hot dish. Over low heat, melt the redcurrant jelly in the sauce, pour into a sauceboat and serve separately. Plain boiled potatoes go best with this dish.

The Secret of good thick gravy: It should be well-reduced after cooking. If it is not, put it into a saucepan and boil up hard, without a lid, for a few minutes, before adding the redcurrant jelly.

RABBIT WITH MUSTARD & CREAM SAUCE

Preparation and cooking: 1 hour

For 4
1 rabbit, cut in joints
1 tablespoon oil
30g/1½oz (*3 Tbsp*) butter or margarine
1 level tablespoon flour
1 onion
3 cloves
½ litre/1 pint (2½ cups) stock
Bouquet garni
1 tablespoon strong mustard
2 tablespoons thick cream
Salt and pepper

1. Quickly brown the rabbit joints in a little very hot oil in a large pan over a high heat.
2. When the meat is nice and brown, transfer it into a saucepan, adding the butter or margarine, still over a high heat. Shake the flour over it, stirring it in with a wooden spoon so that it blends into the mixture.
3. Add the peeled, whole onion with the 3 cloves stuck in it, the bouquet garni, salt and pepper and stock. Cover with a tight-fitting lid and leave to simmer on a very gentle heat for 45 minutes. When the rabbit is cooked, put it in a deep serving dish and keep hot.
4. In a bowl, stir the mustard into the fresh cream. Now beat this gently into the remainder of the gravy in which the rabbit was cooked, over a very low heat. Finally, pour this over the rabbit as soon as the mustard cream has blended in. Serve with plain boiled potatoes or noodles.

The Secret of not curdling the cream and mustard sauce: It should never be brought to the boil. It is even better to stir it into the cooking liquid with the saucepan off the heat. The mixture can always be heated again, without boiling, before pouring over the meat.

RABBIT STEW

Preparation and cooking: 1½ hours

For 4
1 rabbit, weighing 1¼–1½ kg/3lb, cut in joints
2 carrots
1 onion
2 leeks
1 stick celery
Juice of 1 lemon
1 clove
1 clove garlic
Bouquet garni
200 g/8 oz button mushrooms
Salt and pepper

The poulette sauce
1–2 tablespoons flour
30g/1½oz (*3 Tbsp*) butter or margarine
½ litre/1 pint (*1¼ pints*) stock from rabbit
1 egg yolk

1. Peel and dice the vegatables. Cut leeks and celery into fine slices.
2. In a pan, blanch the rabbit joints by bringing cold water to the boil, putting in the rabbit joints and bringing water back to the boil. Then drain and rinse rabbit joints in running cold water.
3. Sprinkle rabbit joints with lemon juice. Place in a flameproof casserole with the vegetables, clove, garlic, bouquet garni and the salt and pepper. Add cold water to cover, bring to the boil and allow to simmer for 45 minutes.
4. Quarter the mushrooms, cook in a saucepan until tender with a few drops of lemon juice and rabbit stock just to cover. Drain mushrooms and reserve the stock.
5. Take out the rabbit joints and drain. Place them, with the mushrooms, in a deep, hot dish.
6. *The poulette sauce*: Over gentle heat stir the flour into the butter. When creamy, pour in the rabbit stock and the stock in which the mushrooms have been cooked. Bring just to boiling point and simmer for 5 minutes. Put the egg yolk in a bowl with several spoonfuls of the hot sauce. Stir, then pour this liaison (thckening) into the casserole off the heat, whisking all the time. Pour over the rabbit just before serving.

The Secret of a really white rabbit stew (blanquette): The rabbit joints are quickly blahched (in paragraph 2) to avoid the greasy scum which tends to form during cooking. Sprinkling with lemon juice also helps.

JUGGED HARE

Preparation and cooking: About 2½ hours
Marinate: 2–3 days

For 6
1 hare
100g/4oz (½ *cup*) butter or margarine
1 tablespoon flour
1 liqueur glass brandy
1 tablespoon tomato paste
250g/10oz streaky bacon
12 button, or pickling, onions
3 slices white bread
400g/16oz button mushrooms
Chopped parsley
Salt and pepper

The marinade
1 litre/1¾ pints (2¼ *pints*) red wine
1 tablespoon oil
3 tablespoons vinegar
1 carrot, chopped
2 shallots, chopped
1 clove garlic, crushed
Bouquet garni
Sage
Tarragon
6 peppercorns
2 cloves

1. *The marinade.* Clean and draw the hare, or ask the butcher to do this for you, and reserve the liver. Catch the blood in a bowl and set aside, mixed with a few drops of vinegar. Trim liver and cut the hare into joints. Put hare pieces and liver into a bowl with all the marinade ingredients. Leave in the refrigerator or a cold place for 2–3 days.
2. *Cooking.* Drain the meat well and set aside the liver. Lightly brown meat with the vegetables from the marinade. Dust with flour. Mix in, then sprinkle over with the brandy. Set alight over a high heat. When the flames have subsided, add tomato paste, salt, pepper and just enough of the marinade liquid to cover. Simmer for about 2 hours over a very low heat.
3. Cut the bacon into strips and bring to the boil in water to cover. Drain. Lightly brown with the onions in 30g/1½oz (*3 Tbsp*) of butter. Cover halfway through the cooking.
4. Cut each slice of bread diagonally to form four triangles. Fry them until crisp in 40g/1½oz (*3 Tbsp*) butter.
5. Strain the sauce from the meat, and keep the meat hot on a serving dish. Replace the sauce on the heat with the bacon and onions and boil up for a few minutes.

6. Meanwhile, in another pan, quickly sauté the mushrooms in the rest of the butter and add them to the meat. Remove the sauce from the heat and gradually blend into it the hare's blood, stirring all the time. Pour this over the hare. Dip the corners of the bread croûtes in the sauce and then into the chopped parsley (the sauce makes it stick to the bread) and arrange around the jugged hare on the edge of the serving dish. Serve with boiled potatoes or plain buttered noodles.

Note: Dried mushrooms may be used instead of fresh. Remember to soak them before cooking.

The Secret of achieving a really rich sauce: Put liver and blood through a blender. Add brandy and, if wished, 2–3 tablespoons thick cream. Add a spoonful of hot sauce from the pan to the blood. Then pour into the remaining sauce stirring continuously over a low heat. Don't allow to boil or the blood will coagulate.

MAIN COURSE DISHES: FISH AND SHELLFISH

Fish, in France, says Françoise Bernard, has gained a somewhat melancholy reputation, due no doubt to its association with Lent, with meatless days and the fact that it is easily digested by those on an invalid diet. In fact, France – for the size of its population, consumes less fish per head than most other European countries. This is surprising when you see the variety of ways in which it can be presented. It is usually poached first in the classic 'court-bouillon' or fish stock to add savour, and served with a creamy sauce.

We include recipes for shellfish too, one or two of which have been very slightly adapted as they call for the French 'langouste' or crawfish, not easily found in Britain. Scampi or Dublin Bay prawns can be used instead and as these are available frozen, this removes the time-consuming chore of shelling them.

CHOOSING FISH

The eye of a fish on a slab never lies. Look at it closely. If it is sunken, dull and lustreless, that's a bad sign. If it looks prominent, transparent – the fish is fresh. The skin should look shiny, the scales firm, and not be shedding. Oily fish such as herrings, mackerel and red mullet is generally stiff when fresh, not flaccid or slack; white fish such as whiting, haddock, hake or cod, is often soft. If you are not sure, lift back the gills and inspect the inside. It should be pink and odourless. There is no substitute, however, for being on good terms with your local fishmonger . . .

Allow 120–150g/5–6oz filleted fish per person; 250–300g/9–12oz whole fish per person.

PREPARATION OF FISH

If your fishmonger cannot be persuaded to do this for you, you will have to clean, and gut the fish. Clean a round fish by slitting skin from below the head, down the belly to the tail. Scrape out dark gut and any dark parts of flesh. If this does not come away easily, rub with rock salt. It should detach more easily. Clean a flat fish, such as plaice or sole, by making a crescent-shaped cut on the underside below the head. Scrape out the gut.

Wash fish thoroughly in running water, and dry with absorbent kitchen paper, or a kitchen cloth which can then be washed.

It can be kept in the coldest part of the refrigerator near the ice-box for 1–2 days only. Wrap in foil to prevent the flavour transferring to other dishes. *Do not try to keep fish fresh in a bowl of water.* Without a refrigerator, it is safe to keep for a few hours, and should always be eaten on the day of purchase. Keep, wrapped, in a cool, airy place, and do not unwrap until the last moment. The less you touch it, the better it will keep. Only when the weather is thundery, should you clean and gut it straightaway. After gutting and cleaning, sponge with vinegar, sprinkle with salt and wrap in a clean kitchen cloth.

COURT-BOUILLON (FISH STOCK) FOR POACHING FISH

For large and medium-sized fish, bring to the boil 2 litres/$3\frac{1}{2}$ pints ($4\frac{1}{2}$ *pints*) water, with 5 tablespoons vinegar, 2 onions, peeled and sliced, a clove, 1 shallot, peeled, 1 bouquet garni and salt and pepper to taste. Boil for 15 minutes, and allow to cool.

Immerse fish to be cooked in the court bouillon, and put on a low heat. Just as boiling point is reached, take pan off heat. Allow fish to cool in the stock for about 12 minutes. If the fish is to be eaten cold, allow to cool completely in the stock.

Note: Lemon juice can be substituted for the vinegar.

Quick method: For a quick stock, use only half as much water and, when it has cooked, add cold water to make up the required amount. This ensures that it is now at the right temperature to cook the fish, and still adequately flavoured.

The Secret of firmly-cooked fish: It should never be allowed to boil in the stock, or the flesh will tend to break up. Not matter what size, if it is brought to the boil slowly and then cooled, it will be thoroughly cooked.

GRILLING FISH

For medium-size and small fish.

If the fish weigh more than 200g/$\frac{1}{2}$lb, prick the skin more deeply to ensure it is cooked right through. (A very big fish would be cut in slices.) Coat with cooking oil. Place the fish on a very hot grill (broiler) and turn over halfway through cooking.

The Secrets of grilling whole fish to keep it soft and fully flavoured: All fish for grilling, whether whole or steaks should be left to marinate in a little lemon juice, 2–3 tablespoons oil and fresh or dried herbs for a good half hour before cooking.

Thicker fish are often grilled to start with, then finished off in the oven to stop them becoming too moist.

Use a palette knife or spatula to turn them as they break very easily.

FRYING FISH 'MEUNIÈRE'

For medium or small fish or fish steaks. (Slit the skin along the dorsal fin to aid cooking if the fish is thick.)

Immerse the fish in milk to cover. Season with salt and pepper. Remove and sprinkle lightly with flour. Place the fish in a large frypan or skillet, containing half oil to half butter, and cook over moderate heat for 8–12 minutes (depending on size). Turn the fish over during cooking. Use a large enough pan so that the whole fish touches the bottom. Non-stick pans are ideal for cooking fish. If you cannot cook all the fish at the same time, transfer each cooked fish to a slow oven (Gas Mark 1, 275°F, 130°C) the moment it is done. Make sure that there is enough cooking oil or fat in the pan before cooking. This should help stop the fish from sticking, rather than adding more fat during cooking. Shake the pan before turning the fish rather than stirring the fish round with a fork, as this can break up the flesh.

The Secret of cooking more fish than the pan will hold at one time: It's simply a matter of organization. Cook the first fish just until it is crispy golden on each side before popping it into the oven, where it will continue to cook a little. The second fish should be kept fractionally longer in the pan, and each subsequent fish fried just that little bit longer than its predecessor. In this way when the last fish is put into the oven, they should all be equally cooked.

COD WITH RUSSIAN SALAD

Preparation and cooking: 45 minutes
Leave for 1 hour before serving

For 4–5
1kg/2¼lb cod

The court-bouillon
2 litres/3½ pints (4½ *pints*) water
4–5 tablespoons vinegar
2 onions, sliced
1 shallot, peeled
1 clove
Bouquet garni
Salt and pepper

The Russian salad
1 large can chopped mixed vegetables (diced carrots, potatoes, turnips, French beans, and peas)
½ pint mayonnaise (*see page 29*) – or ready-made
1 tin anchovy fillets

1. *The court-bouillon.* Boil the water, with the vinegar, onions, salt and pepper, shallot, clove and bouquet garni for 15 minutes. Leave to cool. Place the fish in the stock and bring it slowly back almost to boiling point, then remove it from the heat without boiling. Leave fish to cool in the stock.
2. Soak anchovy fillets in milk or warm water to remove excess salt. Pour the vegetables into a strainer in good time for them to drain completely. Just before use coat them with 2 tablespoons of the mayonnaise.
3. Drain the fish and remove the skin by scraping it gently. Place the fish on a long serving dish.
4. *To serve.* Arrange spoonfuls of the diced vegetables on either side of the fish. Decorate the top of the fish with a criss-cross pattern of anchovies and mayonnaise. Serve the rest of the vegetables in a salad bowl.

The Secret of cooking a whole large fish without a fish kettle: (which is very useful for cooking large fish, but a bit cumbersome to keep for occasional use). Substitute a large kitchen cloth or piece of white linen. Wrap the fish in this completely and tie at both ends before immersing in the stock. After cooking, be careful when lifting out to avoid accidents.

STUFFED FILLETS OF SOLE

Preparation and cooking: 45 minutes   Main course or starter

For 4
9 sole fillets
2 tablespoons thick cream
1 small egg white
200g/8oz button mushrooms
2 tablespoons white vinegar
1 glass white wine
20g/scant oz (*2 Tbsp*) butter
20g/scant oz (*2 Tbsp*) flour
Salt and pepper

Thin string for tying

1. Take one fish fillet and pound into a purée, using a pestle and mortar or a liquidizer. Add one tablespoon thick cream, one small egg white and season with salt and pepper and mix together.
2. Place a spoonful of this stuffing on each of the remaining 8 fillets and roll up, from tail to head end. Tie firmly with thin string. Wash mushrooms in about $\frac{1}{2}$ litre/1 pint (*1$\frac{1}{4}$ pints*) water, with 2 tablespoons vinegar, and cut in fine slices. Place at the bottom of a lightly-buttered gratin dish, put the rolled fillets on top, add the white wine and cover dish with kitchen foil. Cook in a moderate oven (Gas Mark 5–6, 375–400°F, 185°C) for 15–20 minutes.
3. Remove fillets and drain them; remove the string. Arrange the fillets on a hot serving dish and keep warm. Turn the cooking juices and mushrooms into a pan. Cook over high heat and add the butter, mixed into the same amount of flour, little by little to thicken the sauce. Allow to boil for a moment or two, stirring continuously. Take pan off heat and the moment the bubbles subside, add the other tablespoon of thick cream. Pour over the sole fillets. If cooking as a main dish, serve with creamed potatoes, plain boiled rice and a green vegetable, or salad of your choice.

This recipe is equally good when plaice is substituted for sole.

The Secret of stuffed sole which stays stuffed: Tying up the fillets before cooking. Then they do not uncurl in the oven.

MACKEREL WITH GARLIC

Preparation and cooking: 35 minutes

For 4
8 small or 4 medium mackerel
40g/2oz (*4 Tbsp*) butter or margarine
15 cloves garlic
1 lemon
Salt and pepper

1. Put the cloves of garlic, unpeeled, into a small pan of boiling water for 2–3 minutes. Drain, peel and lightly crush them on the bottom of an ovenproof gratin dish. Arrange cleaned and gutted mackerel on top. Season with salt and pepper and dot with butter or margarine.
2. Put into a hot oven (Gas Mark 7, 425°F, 220°C) for about 20 minutes. Serve fish from the dish in which they were cooked, garnished with slices of lemon, with plain boiled potatoes.

The Secret: It is such a simple dish that it can hardly fail. Adjust the quantity of garlic if you wish.

RED MULLET 'EN PAPILLOTE'

Preparation and cooking: 40 minutes   Main course or starter

For 4
4 red mullet
250g/9oz mushrooms
1 shallot, peeled
50g/2oz (*4 Tbsp*) butter or margarine
1 cup milk
A little flour
Oil (see method)
Salt and pepper

Foil

1. Wash mushrooms and chop them finely with the peeled shallot. Cook them, uncovered, in half the butter or margarine with a little salt and pepper until the liquid made by the mushrooms evaporates. Stir from time to time with a wooden spoon.
2. Dip the cleaned fish (gutted or whole) into milk, seasoned with salt and pepper and then into the flour. Melt the rest of the butter and 2 tablespoons oil and cook over a moderate heat for about 5 minutes on each side.
3. *The papillotes.* Cut four large squares of foil – much larger than the fish. Brush well with oil. Arrange a quarter of the mushrooms and one fish on each. Bring up the sides of foil over the fish, rolling the edges together to form a roomy, completely sealed envelope.
4. Just before serving, put into a hot oven (Gas Mark 7, 425°F, 220°C) for about 5 minutes. Serve immediately.

Variation: The mushrooms may be replaced by anchovy paste mixed with butter. In this case add pepper but no salt.

The Secret of preventing butter from burning: The oil which is added to the pan will prevent the butter from browning too quickly, and burning in the pan during cooking.

RED MULLET WITH HERBS

Preparation and cooking: 45 minutes

For 4
4 large red mullet
30g/1½oz (*3 Tbsp*) butter or margarine
Olive oil (see method)
1 onion, sliced
1 clove garlic
Rosemary (fresh or dried)
1 lemon
4 pinches saffron or powdered ginger
½ glass dry white wine
Salt and pepper

1. Marinate the whole fish for at least 15 minutes in a little olive oil, with the sliced onion, garlic, a sprig or two of fresh rosemary (or a pinch or two of dried herbs), and the juice of ½ lemon. Cover the dish with a lid or a sheet of kitchen foil.
2. Lightly butter inside a gratin dish and place the mullet in it side by side. Pour over the marinade. Add salt, pepper and saffron or ginger. Slice the rest of the lemon and place in the dish. Dot the surface of the fish with the butter or margarine and pour in the white wine. Cook in a very hot oven (Gas Mark 8, 450]F, 230]C) for about 25 minutes.

Serve with plain boiled potatoes and a green vegetable, or salad.

The Secret of serving whole red mullet: This fish, considered by some to be the very finest, has few bones, apart from the backbone, which is very easily removed when the fish is cooked.

FISH PAUPIETTES IN CREAM

Preparation and cooking: 25 minutes

For 4
4 fillets firm white fish (haddock, sole, plaice, brill)
Fresh or dried tarragon (see method)
2–3 tablespoons vinegar
Bouquet garni
Salt and pepper

The sauce
1 (2) tablespoons flour
30g/1½oz (*3 Tbsp*) butter or margarine
¼ litre/½ pint (1¼ *cups*) court-bouillon *(see page 139)*
2–3 tablespoons thick cream, or 1 egg yolk

4 *cocktail sticks or fine string*

1. Sprinkle fish fillets with salt and pepper. Place 3 sprigs of fresh tarragon (or 2 pinches dried tarragon) in the centre of each, roll up and secure with a cocktail stick, or with the thread.
2. Place fish 'paupiettes' tightly packed, in a deep saucepan, add water to cover, add 2–3 tablespoons vinegar and tuck the bouquet garni into the dish. Bring slowly to the boil over low heat, then turn off heat.
3. *The sauce*. In a pan over low heat, stir the flour into the melted butter and when slightly cooked, add the court-bouillon. Stir until the sauce thickens, and simmer gently for a further 10 minutes. Add 2–3 tablespoons thick cream, or draw pan from heat and stir in the egg yolk.
4. Drain the paupiettes and remove the cocktail sticks, or thread. Place on a warm serving dish and pour the sauce over. Serve immediately with plain boiled rice, or creamed potatoes.

The Secret of fish fillets that are easy to roll up: Dip the blade of a kitchen knife in water and stretch out each fillet, with long strokes of the flat of the blade. Always roll up from the narrower end.

TROUT IN WHITE WINE

Preparation and cooking: 30 minutes

For 4
4 trout
2 glasses dry white wine
25g/1oz (*2 Tbsp*) butter
1 level tablespoon flour
1 lemon
Salt and pepper

1. Gut and wash the trout, drying them with absorbent kitchen paper. Lay them close together in an ovenproof gratin dish and season them. Add the wine and put in a hot oven (Gas Mark 7, 425°F, 220°C) for 10 minutes.
2. Pour the liquid in which the fish has been cooked into a saucepan.
3. Put the saucepan on moderate heat. Knead together the butter and flour and add it, a little at a time, to the sauce. Stir continuously until boiling, and allow to boil for a few minutes until the sauce thickens a little. Adjust seasoning. Cut two lemon rings and squeeze the rest of the juice into the sauce. Pour this over the trout and put half a lemon ring on the head of each fish to garnish before serving. The dish is usually served with boiled new potatoes.

Variation: You can use the same recipe for a large salmon trout, in which case the cooking time will be longer (about 20 to 25 minutes).

Two teaspoons of thick, fresh cream can be added to the sauce off the heat but be careful as this can curdle with the lemon.

The Secret of trout which does not lose it shape in cooking: It should be gutted through the gills and not by slitting open the body. Ask the fishmonger to do this for you.

TROUT WITH CHIVES

Preparation and cooking: 40 minutes

For 4
4 trout
25g/1oz (*2 Tbsp*) butter
1 shallot, finely chopped
2 glasses dry white wine, or water
1-2 tablespoons snipped chives
Juice of ½ a lemon
4 tablespoons thick cream
Salt and pepper

1. Lightly butter an ovenproof gratin dish. Sprinkle the chopped shallot over the bottom. Clean and gut trout, and lay on top; add the white wine, 1-2 tablespoons snipped chives, salt and pepper and the juice of ½ a lemon. Cook in a very hot oven (Gas Mark 8, 450°F, 220°C) for 10 minutes.
2. Remove trout and drain on absorbent kitchen paper. Transfer to a warm serving dish and keep hot. Turn the cooking juices into a small saucepan, add the cream and stir until boiling. Allow to boil for a minute or two to thicken the sauce a little. Pour over the trout and serve at once, with plain boiled potatoes sprinkled with chopped parsley.

The Secret of trout which do not split apart after cooking: See recipe for *Trout in White Wine*. Clean carefully without opening right up. They will be more attractive to serve.

LOTTE 'EN MATELOT'

Preparation and cooking: 1 hour

For 4
1kg/2¼lb lotte (angler fish) or any firm-fleshed white fish (e.g. cod, turbot, rock salmon)
2–3 tablespoons flour
50g/2oz (*4 Tbsp*) butter or margarine
2 glasses red wine
10 button or pickling onions, peeled
Bouquet garni
125g/6oz mushrooms
Salt and pepper

1. Cut the white fish into pieces, season with salt and pepper and dip in flour.
2. In a flameproof casserole, heat the butter or margarine. Put in the fish pieces and cook over high heat, until golden on all sides. Add the wine, a glass of water, the onions, bouquet garni, and adjust seasoning. Cover the casserole and allow to simmer over gentle heat for 45 minutes. Wash and chop the mushrooms. Add them to the dish 10 minutes before the end of cooking time.
3. Remove pan from heat and drain the pieces of fish. Keep warm in a deep serving dish. Remove the bouquet garni from the sauce and boil rapidly for 5 minutes. Pour over the fish and serve.

The Secret of keeping the sauce red instead of brown: A red wine sauce will take on the colour of an old violin, so add a little tomato paste before serving to make it took more appetizing.

SALMON WITH MOUSSELINE SAUCE

Preparation and cooking: 1 hour
Standing time: 30 minutes

For 10 or 12
1 fresh or frozen salmon weighing 3kg/7lb
1 bottle dry white wine
2 onions
2 carrots
Bouquet garni
2 lemons
Parsley
Salt and pepper

The mousseline sauce
5 egg yolks
2 lemons
250g/10oz (1¼ *cups*) butter
5 tablespoons thick cream
Salt and pepper

1. Boil in a fish kettle or large saucepan: 2 litres/3½ pints (*4 pints*) of water, the white wine, onions and carrots sliced into rings, the bouquet garni, salt and pepper. Leave to cook for 30 minutes. Allow to cool. Place the salmon on the fish kettle grill and immerse in this cold stock. Bring slowly back to the boil and leave to simmer gently for 10 minutes.
2. *The mousseline sauce.* Put the egg yolks, salt and pepper and the juice of 1 lemon in a deep frypan or skillet. Whisk vigorously over very low heat until the mixture begins to thicken and stick to the blades of the beater. Make sure that the sides of the pan are never so hot that they cannot be touched. Remove from the heat. Add the butter a little at a time, and the juice of the second lemon, stirring continuously. Keep warm. Lightly whip the cream and fold into the sauce.
3. *To serve.* Carefully skin the fish, except for the head. Put it in a serving dish on a folded white napkin to absorb the liquid. Garnish with lemon rings and chopped parsley. Serve with boiled new potatoes and hand the mousseline sauce separately.

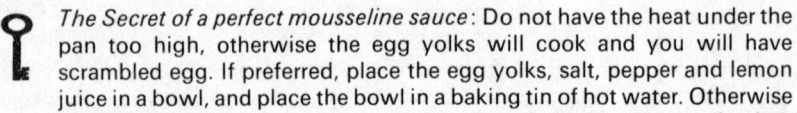

The Secret of a perfect mousseline sauce: Do not have the heat under the pan too high, otherwise the egg yolks will cook and you will have scrambled egg. If preferred, place the egg yolks, salt, pepper and lemon juice in a bowl, and place the bowl in a baking tin of hot water. Otherwise use a double boiler. The sauce should be buttery, light and smooth when finished.

SALMON IN ASPIC

Preparation and cooking: 2 hours — Cold party dish

For 10–12
1 fresh or frozen salmon, weighing 3kg/6–7lb

The court-bouillon
2 litres/3½ pints (4½ *pints*) water
1 bottle dry white wine
2 carrots, sliced
2 onions, sliced
Bouquet garni
Salt and pepper

The decoration
2 sachets aspic powder (makes 2 pints)
1 tomato, skinned and sliced
1 hard-boiled egg
1 leek, sliced

1. *The court-bouillon.* Boil up the water in a fish kettle or large saucepan for 30 minutes, with the wine, sliced carrots and onions, bouquet garni, salt and pepper. Leave to cool. Plunge the salmon into the court-bouillon; the fish should be completely covered. Bring gently to the boil and leave to simmer for 10 minutes. Allow it to cool in the liquid.
2. Prepare the aspic jelly according to instructions on the packet. Pour a thin layer over the base of a long, oval serving dish. Leave to set.
3. Carefully drain the fish and place on a serving dish. Brush fish well with cool, liquid aspic. Dip slices of tomato and leek in the cool aspic and use to decorate the fish. Chop the egg white into neat cubes, and place on the fish, before brushing the whole again with liquid aspic. Allow the rest of the aspic to set, then surround the salmon with chopped cold aspic jelly.

The Secret of cooling aspic jelly: Place bowl of aspic, made up according to the directions on the packet, over a bowl of ice-cubes. Spoon, chilling each spoonful first, slowly over the fish. If the aspic sets too quickly, transfer to a small pan and reheat for a few seconds.

CHOOSING SHELLFISH

Shellfish are bought alive, cooked, or frozen. Live shellfish, mussels, crab etc., should be heavy and tightly-closed. This is proof that they are fresh as they still retain water. Occasionally they may open up because of the weather – touch them and they should snap shut immediately. If not, discard immediately. However, when in doubt, don't buy. The smell will usually be enough to judge by. . . .

Do not keep shellfish for more than a few hours, even in a refrigerator. If you do, cook in a court-bouillon (*see page 139*), but even so, this only gives you a further 24 hours in the refrigerator.

Scallops – are often sold in the half shell, which can be an advantage, but smell them first to make sure they are fresh.

Oysters – which are still alive react by contracting when you touch them or squeeze lemon juice on to them. Once open, they should last for 2–3 hours in a not-too-cold fridge.

Mussels – Fresh mussels should be heavy. Flick them with your fingernail; they should not sound hollow. Don't buy broken or open mussels, and those that don't open in cooking should be thrown away.

The recipes in this section are for main course dishes. Further recipes for shellfish are to be found in the *Starters* section, beginning on page 15.

Crabs – are best poached and eaten plain, with mayonnaise. Never put a fresh crab in fresh water, as it will soon die.

Prawns and shrimps – should be pale pink in appearance. Those that are bright red have probably been artificially coloured with food colouring.

Lobsters – should always be bought live for use in hot dishes and the fishmonger should kill them for you. Cook as soon as possible after this. Otherwise, the lobster is killed painlessly if you place it on a chopping board, hold it in a kitchen cloth just behind the head and drive a sharp knife or skewer straight between the eyes, through the cross mark in the middle of the head. Plunge at once into boiling water.

CRAB MATATOU

Preparation and cooking: 2½ hours

For 4
4 medium-size crabs (weighing about 400g/1lb each, with shell)
4 slices white bread
½ glass dry white wine
50g/2oz (*4 Tbsp*) butter
150g/5oz minced raw pork
4 spring onions (scallions) or 2 button or pickling onions
1 clove garlic
1 small green pepper (pimiento)
2 (*3*) tablespoons breadcrumbs
Salt and pepper

The court-bouillon
1 wine glass vinegar
1 carrot, sliced
1 onion, sliced
3 cloves
Bouquet garni
10 white peppercorns

1. Boil the crabs in the court-bouillon ingredients for about 15 minutes, then leave to cool in the liquid.
2. Remove claws and undershell. Set aside. Remove all the brown and white meat from the crab and set aside. Be sure to discard the small sac at the top of the big shell, any greenish matter and the sponge-like lungs. Crack the claws and pincers and remove meat. Soak the bread in the white wine.
3. Finely chop the white part of the spring onions (scallions), or onions with the garlic and pimiento. Cook them in the butter or margarine together with the minced pork until the onions are transparent. Now add the crab meat, the drained and crumbled bread and season with salt and pepper.
4. Fill the crab shells with this mixture. Sprinkle with breadcrumbs and dot with a little extra butter or margarine. Slide under the grill (broiler) or into the top of a hot oven (Gas Mark 7, 425°F, 215°C) to brown.

The Secret of removing every scrap of crab meat: Use a teaspoon for the body shell, and a skewer for the claws. Then you can get every particle.

SCALLOPS IN PASTRY SHELLS

Preparation and cooking: 40 minutes

For 4
12–16 scallops (depending on size)
A little flour
40g/1½oz (*3 Tbsp*) butter
1 clove garlic
1 shallot, chopped
1–2 tablespoons chopped parsley
Salt and pepper

The shortcrust pastry (for 4 shells)
150g/5oz (*1 heaped cup*) flour
½ teaspoon salt
75g/3oz (⅓ *cup*) butter or margarine
Ice-cold water to mix

8 empty scallop shells

1. *The shortcrust pastry.* Mix together flour, salt and butter or margarine (cut in pieces) with your fingertips. When the mixture looks like fine breadcrumbs, add just enough ice-cold water to form a firm dough. Knead quickly and roll into a ball. Flatten with the palm of your hand and re-form into a ball. Repeat twice more. If possible, leave in the refrigerator to chill for a short time before rolling out. Lightly butter the insides of four of the scallop shells. Roll out the pastry and lay it on top of the shells, press it well in, then trim the edges so that the shells are lined with pastry (*a*). Press in again and place a second shell on top to act as a similarly-shaped weight (*b*). Bake in a hot oven (Gas Mark 7, 425°F, 220°C) for 10 minutes. Halfway through cooking, remove the top shells.
2. Clean the scallops, keeping only the white 'nut' of flesh and the orange coral. Roll lightly in flour, sauté for 6–7 minutes in a frypan or skillet with the remaining butter, over a high heat. Add the chopped garlic, shallot, parsley, salt and pepper while cooking.
3. Turn out the pastry cases. Fill with the scallop mixture and the juices from the pan. Serve immediately, with a green or mixed salad.

The Secret of well-formed pastry shells: The second shell placed on top of the uncooked pastry and fitting into the lower shell keeps the shape during cooking. However, in order to lightly brown the top of the pastry, don't forget to remove the second shell once the pastry is firm enough.

A

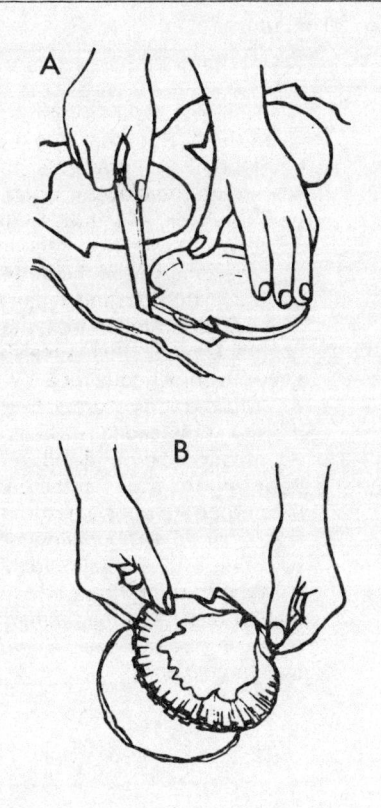

B

SCALLOPS IN CREAM SAUCE

Preparation and cooking: 30 minutes

For 4
16 scallops

The court-bouillon
Bouquet garni
2 shallots, chopped
1 onion (peeled but left whole)
2 cloves
2 glasses dry white wine
2 glasses water
Salt and pepper

The sauce
30g/1½oz (*3 Tbsp*) butter or margarine
1 tablespoon flour
2 egg yolks
2 tablespoons thick cream

1. Remove scallops from shells and carefully clean them. Put them into a saucepan with the court-bouillon ingredients (the onion should be stuck with the cloves). Bring very slowly to the boil. Cook for 3–4 minutes without boiling. Drain scallops and keep hot, reserving the liquid.
2. *The sauce.* Melt the butter or margarine in a pan, stir in the flour and, when creamy, stir in a cup of the court-bouillon from the scallops. Stir until just thickening – this sauce should be fairly thin. Leave to cook gently for a few minutes.
3. Mix the egg yolks and fresh cream together in a bowl. Take sauce off heat, add a little of the warm sauce to the egg and cream mixture and stir. Pour into the sauce in the pan and, whisking or beating continuously, return to a low heat for a few seconds without allowing to boil or the egg will cook. The sauce should thicken slightly. Pour a little into the bottom of a heated entrée (vegetable) dish. Add the drained scallops and pour remaining sauce over. Serve accompanied by plain boiled rice.

The Secret of firm moist scallops: They must never be allowed to boil but just tremble on the brink of boiling for 3–5 minutes, according to their thickness. Too rapid or too long cooking makes them tough.

SCALLOPS ST JACQUES MORNAY

Preparation and cooking: 1 hour

For 4
12 scallops
1 glass dry white wine
1 onion, sliced
1 clove
Bouquet garni
250g/9-10oz mushrooms
30g/1½oz (*3 Tbsp*) butter
Juice of ½ lemon
25g/1oz (*1 cup*) breadcrumbs
Salt and pepper

The sauce
1-2 tablespoons flour
30g/1½oz (*3 Tbsp*) butter or margarine
2 cups cooking liquid (see method)
1-2 tablespoons thick cream
1 egg yolk
Salt and pepper

4 empty scallop shells

1. Carefully clean the scallops, keeping the 'nut' of white meat and the coral. Bring slowly to the boil in a large saucepan containing the white wine, 1 glass of water, the onion, clove, bouquet garni and salt and pepper. Allow to simmer, just below boiling point, for 3-4 minutes.
2. Wash the mushrooms and finely slice. Cook for 5 minutes, in a frypan or skillet, in the butter with a tablespoon of water, a squeeze of lemon juice and salt and pepper.
3. *The sauce.* Melt the butter over a low light, stir in the flour and cook until creamy. Add 2 cups of the cooking liquid from the scallops and any juice from the cooked mushrooms. Stir until boiling, then adjust the seasoning. Allow to simmer for a further 5 minutes. Add the thick cream, then draw pan from heat and carefully stir in the egg yolk.
4. Pour a little sauce into the bottom of each scallop shell, place 4 scallops on each, add a quarter of the cooked mushrooms, cover with the rest of the sauce and sprinkle with breadcrumbs. Dot each with a little extra butter and slide into a very hot oven (Gas Mark 7, 425°F, 220°C) for a few minutes to brown the tops.

Serve with puréed potatoes, sprinkled with parsley or plain boiled rice.

The Secret of thickening the sauce without curdling: Make sure the sauce has cooled a little before adding the egg yolk. If the sauce is too hot when the egg is added, it will cook or 'scramble'. If, despite your best efforts, this happens, whisk the sauce in a blender for a few seconds.

STUFFED SHELLFISH

Preparation and cooking: 30 minutes (in advance) + 10 minutes before the meal

For 4
6 dozen mussels or 4 dozen large oysters

The stuffings
175g/6oz (¾ *cup*) butter
1 finely-chopped shallot
150g/5oz fresh white breadcrumbs
Chopped parsley
Salt and pepper
or
100g/4oz (½ *cup*) butter
2 cloves garlic, chopped
1 teaspoon curry powder
Juice of ½ lemon
Salt and pepper

1. Scrub the shellfish shells under running water, remove the hairy 'beards' from the mussels and rinse again twice. Open up shells with a knife. Remove empty ones and divide the full shellfish between four individual ovenproof dishes.
2. In a bowl, mix together the ingredients for your chosen stuffing, then put a little of the chosen stuffing on top of the fish in the shell. Chill in the refrigerator until it is time for the meal.
3. Just before serving, slide under the grill (broiler) for 8 to 10 minutes.
   Serve with plain boiled rice.

Note: This dish may be prepared entirely in advance (on the same day) and re-heated.

The Secret of perfect stuffed shellfish: Brown them rapidly under a high heat. If cooked too slowly, they tend to go rubbery.

BAKED LOBSTER

Preparation and cooking: 45 minutes   Hot Starter or Main Course

For 4
2 medium-size lobsters
2 tablespoons oil
Thyme
1 ground bay leaf
30g/1½oz (*3 Tbsp*) butter
1 tablespoon thick cream
Pinch of cayenne
Salt and pepper

1. Have the fishmonger kill the lobsters for you, or kill them painlessly by placing on a chopping board and driving a skewer or sharp knife through the cross mark in the centre of the head.
2. Plunge them directly into boiling salted water until they turn pink (30–40 minutes). Take out.
3. Split the lobsters lengthwise from head to tail. Take out the dark thread, or intestine from the tail, and remove the sac of weed from inside the head. Set aside the coral, and the juice in a bowl.
4. Arrange lobster on a baking tray, shell-side down. Brush generously with oil. Sprinkle with salt, pepper, thyme and ground bay leaf. Put into a hot oven (Gas Mark 8–9, 450–475°F, 230–240°C) for 20 to 25 minutes. Brush with oil again during cooking.
5. Before serving, fork the drained coral into the butter, cream and a pinch of cayenne. Spread over the lobster meat. Replace in the oven for a few seconds, and serve.

Note: English cooks usually remove the large claws before serving.

The Secret of lobster claws which don't dry up: Wrap them in foil halfway through cooking to prevent them cooking much faster than the rest of the lobster.

LOBSTER À L'AMERICAINE

Preparation and cooking: 1¼ hours

For 4
1–1½kg/2½–3lb lobster
3–4 tomatoes
4–5 tablespoons oil
1 carrot
1 shallot
1 liqueur glass brandy
1 tablespoon tomato paste
1½ glasses dry white wine
Bouquet garni with a sprig of tarragon
1 tablespoon flour
2–3 pinches cayenne pepper
25g/1oz (*2 Tbsp*) butter
Mixed fresh or dried herbs
Salt and pepper

1. Ask the fishmonger to kill the lobster or place on a chopping board and kill painlessly by driving a skewer or sharp knife through the cross mark in the centre of the head. Remove the claws. Cut off the head and upper half of the carcass. Chop the tail into five or six slices, removing the dark thread or intestine. Season with salt and pepper. Cut the head in two lengthways and remove the gritty weed sac and discard. Remove creamy meat and coral, and put to one side. Crack the claws. Peel the tomatoes and cut them into quarters.
2. Heat oil in a large frypan or skillet. Add the lobster pieces, including the claws. Redden them quickly over a high heat, remove from pan and keep hot.
3. Chop the carrot and shallot finely and sauté them in the hot oil. Add the lobster pieces and brandy and quickly set alight. When the flame dies down, add the fresh tomatoes, tomato paste, white wine, the same amount of water, the bouquet garni, cayenne pepper and salt and pepper. Leave to boil over high heat for 20 to 30 minutes.
4. Drain and place the pieces of lobster in a hot serving dish. Put the sauce back on to a high heat for a few minutes until the quantity has reduced by a third. Then, little by little, add a large knob of butter kneaded into the flour. Away from the heat, add the soft creamy meat and reserved coral, stir this into the sauce and pour over the lobster pieces.

5. Finally sprinkle with chopped mixed herbs (including tarragon if possible) and serve hot.

This rich dish is usually accompanied by plain boiled rice.

Variation: Prawns, scampi and crayfish can be cooked in exactly the same way.

The Secret of serving Lobster à l'Americaine: Snip across the soft part of the tail shell (underneath each piece of meat) when cooked. This will make the meat easier to detach.

SCAMPI VALENCIENNE

Preparation and cooking: 45 minutes

For 4
½ kilo/1lb scampi or Dublin Bay prawns (fresh or frozen)
Court-bouillon to cover (*see page 139*)
25g/1oz (*2 Tbsp*) butter or margarine
1 onion, chopped
100g/4oz uncooked ham or gammon
1 sweet red pepper (pimiento)
225g/8oz (*1¼ cups*) rice
Bouquet garni
4–5 tablespoons cooked small peas
A few prawns for decoration
Salt and pepper

1. Thaw out frozen scampi at least 12 hours in the refrigerator. Put fresh (or thawed-out) scampi or prawns in a pan, with just enough court-bouillon (*see page 139*) to cover. Bring slowly to the boil, and allow to cook, just below boiling point, for 3 to 4 minutes.
2. In a large saucepan, heat the butter or margarine, add the chopped onion, ham cut into strips and ¾ of the red pepper, cored and de-seeded and cut into shreds. Add the rice, double its quantity of water and the bouquet garni. Adjust seasoning and cook, over medium heat, half-covered, for 17 to 20 minutes.
3. Peel the scampi, and when the rice is cooked, stir in the scampi and peas. Turn out on to a warm serving dish, decorate with the prawns and the rest of the pepper, cut in shreds.

Variation: Pack mixture into a 2-pint (1 quart) mould and turn out on to a hot serving dish. Decorate with scampi and shreds of red pepper.
   Make a white sauce, adding an egg yolk and fresh cream, off the heat, to thicken.

The Secret of peeling fresh scampi easily: With kitchen scissors, cut the underside of the shell from just below the head. Once split, the shell comes off easily. Twist off the head.

PASTA AND RICE

Pasta and rice are becoming ever more popular as alternatives to vegetables to serve with a main course dish. Though you may never try to make your own fresh pasta, you will agree on reading the recipe that it is not difficult. Pasta can be served, with one of the suggested sauces, as a starter or a supper dish. Rice dishes are good for lunch or supper, too, particularly a risotto, such as the one you will find on page 175.

HOME-MADE PASTA

Preparation: several hours   Side dish or supper dish

For 4
200g/½lb *(2 cups)* flour
3 eggs
1 tablespoon cold water
1 level teaspoon salt

For noodles
1.   Heap up the flour and break the eggs into the middle. Add salt and water a little at a time. Fold in the mixture with the fingertips until it is of an elastic consistency, supple but not sticky. Leave to stand.
2.   On a table or worktop, stretch out the dough very thinly on a light, but even, covering of flour.
   Roll up into a roll, lengthwise (*a*).
3.   Slice through the rolled dough at centimetre (½ in) intervals with a very sharp knife (*b*).
4.   Separate the ribbons of dough and stretch out the strands together to dry out for several hours before cooking.

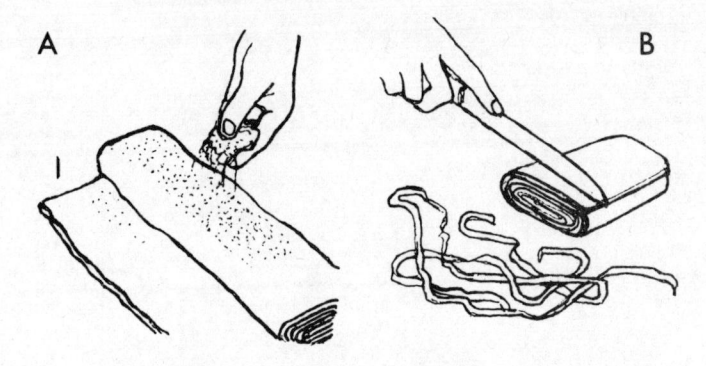

A   B

The Secret of cooking home-made pasta: It cooks very much more quickly than other kinds; only about 2 to 5 minutes maximum in boiling salted water. Drain, flavour and serve immediately.

BOLOGNESE SAUCE

Preparation and cooking: 45 minutes

For 4
300g/12oz minced (ground) steak
50g/2oz raw ham
1 onion
2 cloves garlic
½ carrot
1 stick celery
40g/1½oz (*3 Tbsp*) butter or margarine
1 teaspoon flour
2 tablespoons tomato purée
1 glass red or white wine
Fresh or dried herbs (thyme, rosemary, marjoram, basil)
Salt and pepper

1. Cut the ham into strips and chop the onion, garlic, carrot and celery. Brown the meat in the butter or margarine in a deep flameproof casserole. Shake on the flour, mix together well and add the prepared vegetables, ham, tomato purée, wine, 3 glasses water, herbs, salt and pepper. Simmer uncovered, for 30 minutes. At the end of the cooking time, the sauce should be reduced to half its original quantity.

ITALIAN TOMATO SAUCE

Preparation and cooking: 40 minutes

For 4
50g/2oz bacon, chopped
30g/1½oz (*3 Tbsp*) butter or margarine
2 shallots, chopped
1 clove garlic
1 glass white wine
2 tablespoons tomato purée
Bouquet garni
1 teaspoon flour
Salt and pepper

1. Slightly colour the bacon, shallots and garlic in half the butter or margarine. Add the wine, 2 glasses of water, tomato purée, bouquet garni, salt and pepper. Simmer for 20 minutes. Knead together the flour and the rest of the butter or margarine and add it, bit by bit, to the sauce. Allow to thicken for a few seconds over a low heat. Adjust seasoning and serve with spaghetti, tagliatelle, noodles, etc.

ROQUEFORT NOODLES

Preparation and cooking: 40 minutes   Side dish or hot starter

For 4
250g/8oz noodles
100g/4oz roquefort cheese (see Note)
3–4 tablespoons thick cream
2 cloves garlic
Salt and pepper

1. Cook the pasta in plenty of boiling, salted water.
2. Crumble the cheese in a bowl with a fork. Add the cream and season with pepper.
3. Drain the noodles carefully, and return them to the heat for 1 or 2 minutes with the cheese and cream mixture.
4. Rub the inside of a deep warm serving dish with 2 cut cloves of garlic. Turn the pasta into the dish, mix and serve at once.

Note: If you find roquefort cheese difficult to obtain, you can use Danish blue instead.

The Secret of noodles that do not stick together: Do not allow them to sit in the pan of hot water once they are cooked. Otherwise, they will over-cook and stick together.

MACARONI LANGUEDOC

Preparation and cooking: 45 minutes   Side dish or hot starter

For 4
- 250g/9oz macaroni
- 3 aubergines
- 4–5 tomatoes
- 250g/9oz mushrooms
- 120g/4oz ($\frac{1}{2}$ *cup*) butter or margarine
- 1 clove garlic
- 50g/2oz ($\frac{1}{2}$ *cup*) grated gruyère cheese
- Salt and pepper

1. Peel the aubergines and cut into rings. Sprinkle with salt.
2. Skin, de-seed and chop the tomatoes. Wash and dice the mushrooms.
3. Fry the aubergine rings over a high heat in half the butter or margarine, then add the tomatoes, chopped small, and the garlic clove, salt and pepper. Cover and cook over medium heat for 10 minutes. Add the mushrooms and cook for a further 5 minutes.
4. Meanwhile cook the macaroni in plenty of salted boiling water. Drain it and turn on to a deep dish. Spread over the cooked vegetable mixture, sprinkle with gruyère cheese and dot with butter or margarine. Brown under the grill (broiler) for 10 minutes.

The Secret of preventing the macaroni from boiling over: Soon after the water comes to the boil pour in a few drops of oil.

GNOCCHI ROMANA

Preparation and cooking: 40 minutes   Side dish or hot starter

For 4
125g/5oz ($\frac{2}{3}$ *cup*) coarse semolina
$\frac{1}{2}$ litre/1 pint (1$\frac{1}{4}$ *pints*) milk
30g/1$\frac{1}{2}$oz (*3 Tbsp*) butter
A little nutmeg
1 egg yolk
75g/3oz ($\frac{3}{4}$ *cup*) grated gruyère cheese
A little extra butter
Salt and white pepper

1. Bring the milk to the boil with the butter, a little salt, and 2 pinches of nutmeg. As soon as it boils, pour in the semolina and stir until it thickens. Leave to cook gently for 10 minutes.

2. Draw pan off heat, stir in the egg yolk, three-quarters of the cheese and season with pepper. Leave to cool a little before pouring into a gratin dish rinsed in cold water. Spread out the gnocchi mixture to 1 centimetre ($\frac{1}{2}$-inch) thickness. Allow to get quite cold.

3. Using the rim of a glass or jar, cut out rounds of gnocchi and place on a well-buttered baking sheet. Sprinkle with the rest of the grated cheese and cook in a hot oven (Gas Mark 6, 400°F, 210°C) for 10 to 15 minutes. Serve hot.

The Secret of perfect gnocchi: If you can, make it the day before and leave paste to stiffen overnight before cutting it into rounds.

ITALIAN SEMOLINA

Preparation and cooking: 20 minutes   Side dish

For 4
100g/4oz ($\frac{1}{2}$ *cup*) coarse semolina
1 onion
40g/1$\frac{1}{2}$oz (*3 Tbsp*) butter or margarine
1 stock or bouillon cube
2 tablespoons tomato paste
2 tablespoons grated gruyère cheese
Salt and pepper

1. Finely chop the onion, cook in half the butter or margarine until transparent. Add the semolina and season to taste. Stir, then add 1 pint of boiling stock, made with the bouillon cube. Leave to simmer for 10 minutes.
2. At the end of cooking time, add the tomato paste. When the semolina is completely cooked, mix in the gruyère cheese and the rest of the butter. Serve in a vegetable dish or pack into a mould, and turn out.

The Secret of well turned-out semolina: If using a mould, rinse it in cold water first, before packing in the cooked semolina. It should un-mould perfectly, whether warm or refrigerated.

PLAIN BOILED RICE

Cooking: 15–17 minutes   Side dish

For 4
2 cups rice
Water
Salt

1. Put a large saucepan of salted water on to boil.
2. Rinse the rice in a strainer under fast running cold water.
3. Add it to the boiling water, bring water back to the boil and allow to boil uncovered for 15 to 17 minutes. Taste it as soon as it looks done – the cooking time varies according to quality. As soon as it is cooked, drain and rinse in plenty of cold water to stop any further cooking. If necessary, re-heat in a very low oven or over very gentle heat, with a little butter. Separate the grains with a fork.

Note: A simple way of serving boiled rice is to pack the rice tightly into a medium-size bowl and then turn out on to a plate where it will keep its dome-shape.

The Secret of rice that doesn't boil over during cooking: Add a few drops of cooking oil to the pan of boiling water before putting in the rice.

RICE PILAF

Cooking: 17–20 minutes   Side dish

For 4
225g/8oz (*1¼ cups*) rice
1 onion, chopped
30g/1½oz (*3 Tbsp*) butter or margarine
4 cups water or stock
Bouquet garni
Salt and pepper

1. Wash the rice well in a lot of water, rubbing grains between the palms of the hands. Drain well.
2. In a flameproof casserole, lightly soften the chopped onion in a little butter or margarine. Then add the rice. Mix in so that the grains are well coated with butter, but on no account allow them to brown.
3. Pour the water or stock on the rice. Add the bouquet garni and salt and pepper. Cover tightly and simmer until the liquid is completely absorbed (17 to 20 minutes). The quantity of water can vary slightly according to the type of rice or individual preference – some people like their rice a little hard.

Variation: Pilaf Italian-style: add tomato purée, cooked peas and a little grated cheese, just before the rice has finished cooking.

The Secret of making tasty rice: Use a good meat, fish or vegetable stock, or a bouillon cube and water. Or add a pinch or two of mixed, dried herbs.

SAUTEÉD RICE

Preparation and cooking: 10–20 minutes   Side dish

Use leftover cooked rice and sauté gently in a frypan or skillet with a little butter and other ingredients of your choice. Try these variations:

CREOLE-STYLE: add chopped mushrooms, strips of blanched red or green sweet peppers (pimientos) and slices of tomato.
EGYPTIAN-STYLE: add chopped chicken livers, strips of cooked ham or sautéed mushroom slices.
GREEK-STYLE: add balls of lightly-cooked sausagemeat, cooked peas, red pepper chutney or relish.
MILANAISE-STYLE: add 1–2 pinches saffron, chopped mushrooms and tomato chutney.
INDIAN-STYLE: add curry powder to taste.
HUNGARIAN-STYLE: add diced sautéed onions and paprika.
CANTON-STYLE: add cooked, peeled shrimps and an omelette chopped into strips.
ITALIAN-STYLE: add grated gruyère or parmesan cheese.
LUXEMBOURG-STYLE: serve with two poached eggs on top.

RISOTTO WITH OLIVES

Preparation and cooking: 25 minutes   Main course

For 4
200g/8oz (*1¼ cups*) rice
1 onion
40g/1½oz (*3 Tbsp*) butter or margarine
1 clove garlic
1-2 pinches saffron
Pinch of dried herbs
50g/2oz (*½ cup*) stoned green olives
50g/2oz (*½ cup*) gruyère cheese, grated
Salt and pepper
6 eggs

1. Finely slice the onion, cook until transparent in a flameproof casserole in the butter or margarine. Add the rice and stir. Add 4 cups water, the garlic, saffron, herbs, very little salt (because of the olives) and pepper, cover the pan and bring to the boil. Cook for 17 to 20 minutes over gentle heat.
2. Put the eggs on to hard-boil. Halfway through the cooking time, add the olives to the pan of rice.
3. Adjust the seasoning. Take pan off heat and stir in the cheese. Stir carefully so as not to crush the grains of rice. Serve in a deep dish, surrounded by peeled, hard-boiled eggs cut in half lengthwise.

The Secret of onion-free risotto: If you do not like to find pieces of cooked onion in your finished dish, remove them from the pan before adding the rice. The fat will have absorbed their flavour. In this case, cook rice for a little while longer before adding the water.

VEGETABLES

One of the things that the English have a poor reputation for is cooking vegetables. Anything found on a menu with the words 'à l'Anglaise' usually means plain, boiled and possibly overcooked. The French, being thrifty cooks, are noted for their combinations of vegetables, or for adding a little cooked onion, a herb or two to make them into something special. And we have included one or two recipes using dried vegetables at the end of the section. These take longer to prepare as the peas or beans need soaking overnight for best results. There are very few 'secrets', as vegetables are not difficult to cook.

RÖSTI (SWISS POTATOES)

Preparation and cooking: 1 hour   Vegetable

For 4
800g/1¾lb potatoes
70g/2-3oz (*4-6 Tbsp*) butter or margarine
1 onion, chopped
Salt and pepper

1. Boil the potatoes in their jackets, then peel them when they're cool enough to handle. When they are completely cold, chop them roughly.
2. Melt the butter or margarine in a frypan or skillet and cook the onion until golden and transparent. Add the potatoes, and season with salt and pepper. Stir gently to incorporate all the fat, then pack, without worrying about crushing the potatoes, into a thick 'pancake'. Turn up the heat, and shake the pan to stop the potato cake from sticking.
3. After a few minutes, the edges of the pancakes will be crisp. Slide the potato cake on to a plate, then flip it back into the pan for a further 5 minutes to cook the other side.

Variation: This dish can be made with pre-cooked potatoes, and you can add strips of bacon or slices of cheese at the same time as the onion.

The Secret of peeling potatoes in their jackets: Stick a fork into the hot potato and hold the fork upright while peeling off the skin with a knife.

DAUPHINOIS POTATOES

Preparation and cooking: 1 hour 25 minutes   Vegetable

For 4
1kg/2¼lb potatoes, thinly sliced
1 clove of garlic
30g/1½oz (*3 Tbsp*) butter
50g/2oz (½ *cup*) grated gruyère cheese
Scant ½ litre/¾ pint (*1 pint*) milk
1 egg
Salt and pepper

1. Rub the inside of a large ovenproof gratin dish with garlic (crushed with a pinch of salt) along with half the butter (*a*).
2. Place the very thinly sliced potatoes in layers in the dish and sprinkle half the gruyère cheese between the layers (*b*). Bring three-quarters of the milk to the boil and pour over the potatoes and cheese. Season and cook in a hot oven (Gas Mark 7, 425°F, 220°C) for about 60 minutes.
3. Ten minutes before the potato is cooked, beat up the egg, add salt and pepper and the rest of the milk. Pour this carefully over the potatoes.
4. Sprinkle over the rest of the cheese and dot with the rest of the butter. Lower the oven temperature slightly and replace the dish for several minutes until the mixture 'sets'. Serve immediately with roast or grilled (broiled) red meat.

Note: There are several ways of making this dish: with or without gruyère cheese, with milk, or cream, or half-and-half, and even without garlic... in any event, this particular recipe is guaranteed to succeed.

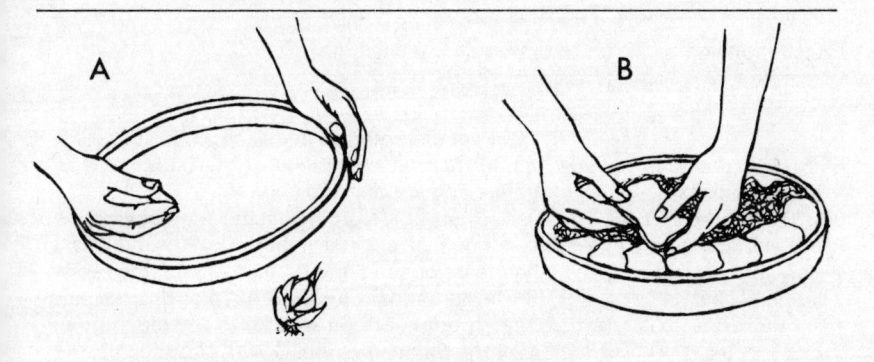

    The Secrets of (1) completely cooked Dauphinois potatoes: The potatoes must be sliced in very thin and equal rounds. This can be done with a special hand grater, called a mandoline which has a single blade on one side, or with a vegetable slicer.

    (2) *How to prevent the milk curdling in cooking*: The milk in a finished dish sometimes looks curdled. In fact, it is merely that the potatoes have produced water while cooking, so we cheat a little. Once the potatoes have cooked, the beaten egg, milk and seasoning is poured on and any liquid from the potatoes is absorbed by the egg into a type of cream.

DOMINO POTATOES

Preparation and cooking: 15 minutes   Vegetable

For 4
800g/1¾lb potatoes, boiled in their jackets
60g/2–2½oz (*4–5 Tbsp*) butter or margarine
1 can (283g/10oz) artichoke hearts
1 can (212g/7½oz) button mushrooms
Chopped parsley
Salt and pepper

1. Peel the potatoes and slice while still warm. Sauté them in two-thirds of the butter or margarine and add salt and pepper.
2. When golden, transfer the potatoes onto a serving dish and keep hot. Cut the artichoke hearts in four and add to the pan with the rest of the butter. Add the mushrooms, well drained, and heat through. Spoon artichokes and mushrooms over the potatoes, sprinkle with chopped parsley and serve immediately.

POTATO GALETTE

Preparation and cooking: 45 minutes   Vegetable

For 4
500g/generous 1 lb potatoes
Oil (see method)
2 eggs, beaten
1 or 2 cloves garlic
2 tablespoons chopped parsley
Salt and pepper

1. Peel potatoes and grate them finely. Rinse under running water to remove starch, drain well and wring in a kitchen cloth to squeeze out as much water as possible.
2. Lightly sauté the potatoes in a little oil, in a large frypan or skillet, for five minutes, just to lightly colour them.
3. Tip the potatoes into a bowl, mix with the beaten eggs, parsley and chopped garlic. Season with salt and pepper.
4. Turn the mixture into a buttered gratin dish and cook in a hot oven (Gas Mark 6–7, 400–425°F, 215°C) for about 15 minutes. Serve hot, with a green salad – or cold for a picnic.

The Secret of cooking lots of grated potatoes in a small pan: Cook in 2 or 3 batches, adding a little more oil between each batch.

POTATO CROQUETTES

Preparation and cooking: 1 hour   Vegetable
(+ several hours in the refrigerator)

For 20 croquettes
500g/1lb potatoes
20g/½oz (*1 Tbsp*) butter or margarine
2 egg yolks
Salt and pepper

The cooking
A little flour (see method)
1 egg
2 egg whites
Breadcrumbs (see method)
50g/2oz (*4 Tbsp*) butter or margarine

1. The evening before if possible, cook the potatoes in their jackets. Peel them and beat into a purée without adding any extra liquid (if necessary, dry them out in the oven for a little longer).
2. Beat in the 20g/½oz (*1 Tbsp*) butter or margarine, the egg yolks, salt and pepper. Beat with a wooden spoon over gentle heat until the mixture resembles choux pastry and does not stick to the sides of the pan. Spread on a large plate in a layer about the thickness of a finger. Chill in the refrigerator.
3. *The cooking.* Form the purée into croquettes (finger-size rolls) and dip them first in the flour, then the lightly-beaten eggs and lastly in the breadcrumbs. Fry lightly, 4 or 5 at a time in a frypan or skillet in melted butter or margarine. Turn them carefully with a spoon so as not to break them, or cook them in a deep fat fryer.

🗝 *The Secret of croquettes which do not split open when cooked*: First, the dryness of the potato purée; second, the hours of chilling in the refrigerator and third, the thick coating, which should be pressed on as carefully as for veal escalopes.

BEETROOT IN CREAM SAUCE

Preparation and cooking: 1½ hours   Vegetable

For 4
1kg/2lb beetroot
1 tablespoon vinegar
50g/2oz (*4 Tbsp*) butter
3–4 tablespoons thick cream
Salt and pepper

1. Boil up some water in a pan, remove any leaves from the tops of the beetroots and slice off the long, thread-like root. Peel beets and cut into dice. Plunge into boiling water, add salt and the tablespoon of vinegar. Allow to boil for about 1 hour.
2. Drain the cooked beetroot very thoroughly, sauté for a few minutes in the butter, then add the fresh cream. Season lightly and cook until the cooking juices have blended with the cream.

Note: Use ready-cooked, peeled beetroot for speed and simply sauté them and add cream.

Variation: Boil beetroots, then in an ovenproof dish, cover them with béchamel sauce (*see page 188*) and grated cheese.

The Secret of peeling beetroot: It is easier to peel cooked beets, so plunge them whole into boiling water, cook for about 1½ hours, then peel. The skin should slip off easily. (Or cheat by buying beetroot ready peeled.)

RED CABBAGE BERNOISE

Preparation and cooking: 1 hour 50 minutes
In a pressure cooker: 35 minutes

Vegetable

For 4
- 1 large red cabbage, at least 1 kg/2lb in weight
- 2 onions
- 100g/4oz bacon, preferably streaky (fat)
- 30g/1½oz (*3 Tbsp*) butter or margarine
- 1 glass red wine
- 2 pinches of nutmeg
- Salt and pepper

1. Peel and cut the onions into rings and de-rind and dice the bacon. Fry both gently in the butter or margarine in a large saucepan, until onions and bacon fat are transparent.
2. Wash the large outer leaves of the cabbage. Roll them up and cut them into fine strips. Quarter the cabbage heart, removing the hard white pieces of stalk, then place the quarters on a chopping board and cut into thin slices. Add the sliced cabbage to the pan and mix with the bacon and onion. Cook for a few minutes, uncovered. Then pour on a glass of red wine, season, and add a pinch or two of nutmeg. Cover pan and simmer for 1½ hours (in a pressure cooker: 35 minutes).

The Secret of braised cabbage which does not stick to itself: A little pork fat (belly of pork) can be put at the bottom of the pan, but it is even better to place a heat diffuser (an asbestos mat, for example) between the base of the pan and the heat source.

CARROTS A LA CRÈME

Preparation and cooking: 1¼ hours　　Vegetable
In a pressure cooker: 25–35 minutes

For 4
1 kg/2 lb carrots
30 g/1½ oz (*3 Tbsp*) butter or margarine
4 button or pickling onions
1 clove garlic
Bouquet garni
1 clove
1–2 tablespoons thick cream
Salt and pepper

1. Scrape and wash the carrots; cut into thin slices.
2. Heat the butter or margarine in a large casserole, add the carrots, onions cut into 4, garlic, bouquet garni, clove, salt and pepper. Cover with a deep saucer filled with water. Cook over low heat for an hour (in a pressure cooker: 25 minutes).
3. Remove the bouquet garni and stir in the fresh cream just before serving.

CARROTS POMPADOUR

Preparation and cooking: about 25 minutes   Vegetable

For 4
500 g/1 lb carrots
500 g/1 lb potatoes
Salt

The béchamel sauce
2 tablespoons flour
40g/1½oz (*3 Tbsp*) butter or margarine
½ litre/1 pint (*2½ cups*) milk
Salt and pepper

1. Scrape and dice carrots and potatoes and cook each separately in boiling salted water for 10–12 minutes.
2. Prepare the béchamel sauce by melting the butter or margarine over a gentle heat, stirring in the flour, and cooking until straw-coloured. Add milk all at once and bring to the boil, stirring continuously with a sauce whisk or wooden spoon. Add salt and pepper and leave to simmer.
3. Drain the vegetables and arrange in a deep serving dish. Pour over the béchamel and serve. (Sprinkle with chopped parsley, if liked.)

CREAMED CAULIFLOWER

Preparation and cooking: 1 hour 20 minutes   Vegetable or hot starter

For 4
1 medium-sized cauliflower
25g/1oz (*2 Tbsp*) butter
50g/2oz ($\frac{1}{2}$ *cup*) grated cheese
3 eggs
Salt

The béchamel sauce
2 tablespoons flour
40g/1$\frac{1}{2}$oz (*3 Tbsp*) butter or margarine
$\frac{1}{2}$ litre/1 pint (2$\frac{1}{2}$*cups*) milk
Nutmeg
Salt and pepper

2-pint capacity soufflé dish

1. Break the cauliflower into sprigs, wash well and cook for 12 to 15 minutes in a pan of boiling salted water.
2. *The sauce*: Melt the butter or margarine over gentle heat, stir in the flour and continue stirring until straw-coloured. Little by little, add the milk and stir over the heat until it thickens. Add salt, pepper and two pinches of nutmeg.
3. Drain the cauliflower and purée in a vegetable mill or blender. Beat in the béchamel sauce and the grated cheese. Separate the eggs, stir in the yolks. Beat the whites until they hold firm peaks, then fold into the cauliflower.
4. Turn into a lightly buttered soufflé dish and cook in a moderate oven (Gas Mark 5–6, 375–400°F, 190–210°C) for 40 minutes. Serve in the dish, straight from the oven. (This dish will not rise, as a cheese soufflé does.)

The Secret of properly cooked cauliflower: Do not leave too long in its cooking liquid, or it will fall apart and not purée well for this dish.

COURGETTES LYONNAISE

Preparation and cooking: 30 minutes   Vegetable

For 4
4 courgettes
3–4 tablespoons oil
2 large onions
20g/¾oz (¾ *Tbsp*) butter or margarine
40g/1½oz (⅓ *cup*) grated gruyère cheese
Salt and pepper

1. Wash and cut courgettes into thick slices – do not peel them. Sauté until golden on both sides in the oil, over high heat. Add salt and pepper; cover and cook gently for 20 minutes.
2. Meanwhile, slice the onions in rounds and cook gently in the butter or margarine, in a separate covered pan for 15 minutes.
3. In an ovenproof gratin dish, place a layer of courgettes, a layer of onions and then the grated cheese. Put into a hot oven (Gas Mark 5, 375°F, 190°C) to melt and slightly brown the cheese.

VENETIAN STYLE RUNNER BEANS

Preparation and cooking: 2 hours
In a pressure cooker: 35 minutes

Vegetable

For 4
1 kg/2 lb runner beans
1 onion
500 g/1 lb tomatoes
60 g/2½ oz (*5 Tbsp*) butter
1 clove garlic
Bouquet garni
2 pinches dried oregano (optional)
1–2 tablespoons chopped parsley
Salt and pepper

1. Top and tail the runner beans and remove any 'strings'. Wash them. Chop the onion, skin, deseed and chop the tomatoes.
2. Melt almost all the butter in a saucepan and in it sauté the onion and tomatoes. Then add the beans and all other ingredients except the parsley. Cover tightly and allow to cook for about 1½ hours (in a pressure cooker: 35 minutes) over very gentle heat.
3. When ready to serve the beans, remove the bouquet garni, add the rest of the butter and sprinkle with parsley.

GLAZED ONIONS

Preparation and cooking: ¾ hour   Vegetable

For 4
350g/12oz button or pickling onions
30g/1½oz (*3 Tbsp*) butter
1–2 tablespoons caster (fine) sugar
Salt

1. Put the onions, unpeeled, into a sieve, plunge it into a pan of boiling water. Allow to boil for 3 minutes then remove from heat. You should be able to peel the onions easily.
2. Put the peeled onions in a pan with the butter and sugar. Cook uncovered until golden – about 30 minutes. Shake the pan from time to time so that they do not stick. The pan may be half-covered for the last quarter of an hour. Season with salt before serving.

The Secret of onions which turn golden without burning: If they colour too quickly, and too much, add 1–2 teaspoons cold water to the pan, and cover with a lid for a while. This should stop them burning.

RATATOUILLE CORDON BLEU

Preparation and cooking: 1¾ hours
In a pressure cooker: 35 minutes

Vegetable or cold starter

For 4
3 onions
4 aubergines
4 courgettes
500g/1lb tomatoes
2 green peppers
1 bulb of fennel (optional)
1 can, 425g/15oz, artichoke hearts
250g/8oz (*1 cup*) oil
2 cloves garlic
Bouquet garni
Salt and pepper

1. Peel and slice onions, aubergines and courgettes. Skin, de-seed and chop tomatoes and peppers and cut fennel into strips.
2. Heat half the oil in a large frypan or skillet. Cook the aubergines and courgettes separately, starting with the aubergines. Transfer them into a flameproof casserole, adding more oil to the frypan. Sauté the courgettes in their turn and add to the casserole, on top of the aubergines. Then cook the tomatoes, peppers and onions together, and add to the casserole. Add the fennel (if using), garlic, bouquet garni and salt and pepper. Cover and allow to simmer over very gentle heat for 1–1½ hours (in a pressure cooker: 30–35 minutes). If the mixture makes too much juice, drain halfway through the cooking time.
3. At the end of cooking, put in the artichoke hearts, each cut in four, for just long enough to heat them through. Serve hot as a vegetable to accompany meat, or it is equally good served cold as a starter.

The Secret of a ratatouille that neither reduces itself to a purée, nor sticks to the bottom of the pan: Sautéing the vegetables separately, then placing them in the casserole in layers without mixing together, prevents them becoming mushy. Aubergines often stick to the pan, so if possible, place a metal grille between the flame and the casserole. Better still, cook the casserole in a moderate oven (Gas Mark 4, 350°F, 175°C) instead of over direct heat.

STUFFED TURNIPS IN CIDER

Preparation and cooking: 1¼ hours   Vegetable or Hot Starter

For 4
4 small round turnips
10g/½oz (*1 Tbsp*) butter
1 wineglass cider
1 stock or bouillon cube

The stuffing
250g/8oz sausagemeat (forcemeat)
1 shallot, chopped
Parsley, chervil, chives
Thyme, bay leaf
1 egg, beaten
Salt and pepper

1. Peel the turnips and scoop out the centres.
2. *The stuffing*: Mix together the sausagemeat, chopped shallot, herbs – fresh or dried – and snipped chives. Bind with the beaten egg and season with salt and pepper. Pile this stuffing into each turnip.
3. Well butter an ovenproof dish. Add salt, pepper, the cider, the stock cube and 4 tablespoons of boiling water. Cover and cook in a hot oven (Gas Mark 6–7, 400 – 425°F, 205 – 215°C) for about 45 minutes.

Note: If possible, use 4 tablespoons of juice from a cooked joint of meat instead of the water and the stock cube in which to braise the turnips. This will add a savoury touch, especially as these stuffed turnips go particularly well with roast veal, pork or a duck, and you use the appropriate juices.

Variation: If you can only find large turnips, cut them in half, and scoop out the centres. Pile up the sausagemeat, and cook as above.

CHICK PEA SALAD

Cooking time: very long
In a pressure cooker: 1½ hours   Cold starter

For 4
400g/1lb chick peas
1 carrot, peeled
1 onion stuck with two cloves
1 clove garlic
Bouquet garni
Salt and pepper

The vinaigrette sauce
Oil and wine vinegar (see method)
1-2 teaspoons mustard
1 tablespoon mixed herbs
1-2 shallots, finely chopped

1. Leave the dried peas to soak in cold water overnight to soften the skins, then place peas in a pan, cover with cold water, bring to the boil and cook for 30 minutes. Drain, cover with plenty of boiling water, add the vegetables then boil for 2-2½ hours until soft. Add salt halfway through the cooking time.
2. Or put them in the pressure cooker with unsalted water. Secure the lid. Boil for 15 minutes, then drain. Put the chick peas back into the pressure cooker with the carrot, onion with cloves, and bouquet garni and cover with boiling water. Lock the lid on the pressure cooker and cook for 45 minutes. Open the pressure cooker, add salt and pepper, and then cook with lid off, for up to a further 45 minutes.
3. *The vinaigrette sauce.* In a bowl, mix together tablespoons of red or white wine vinegar with oil in a proportion of 1 (vinegar) to 3 (oil) and add salt and pepper. Whisk until dressing thickens and add more vinegar and oil until you have about 4fl. oz (½ cup). Add 1 tablespoon chopped mixed herbs, 1 teaspoon strong mustard and the chopped shallots.
4. Drain the peas and rinse them in cold water. Cover them with a good helping of vinaigrette sauce mixed with mustard.

The Secret of tender, tasty chick peas: They have hard skins so when they are cooked, you can remove the skins as you rinse them. This is easily done under running water. Dry them before adding the vinaigrette.

PURÉE ST GERMAIN

Preparation and cooking: Cooking time: 1½ to 2 hours
In a pressure cooker: 5 minutes + 20 minutes   Vegetable

For 4
400g/1lb split peas
50g/2oz streaky bacon
30g/1½oz (*3 Tbsp*) butter
1 carrot
1 onion
A few lettuce leaves
1 cube sugar
Bouquet garni
Salt and pepper

1. Put the peas in a large pan of cold, unsalted water. Bring slowly to the boil. Leave to boil for 15 minutes (in a pressure cooker: 5 minutes), then drain and rinse in cold water.
2. Dice the bacon. Fry in a saucepan with half the butter and add the carrot and onion, cut into rings, together with the split peas, lettuce leaves, sugar, bouquet garni and sufficient boiling water to cover. Cover and leave to cook gently for 1 to 1½ hours (in a pressure cooker: 20 minutes) depending on the texture of the peas. Salt halfway through cooking. If the water evaporates too quickly, add a little more water as needed.
3. Strain the peas but keep the liquid in which they were cooked. Crush them with a vegetable mill or purée in a blender. Add pepper, the rest of the butter and a little cooking stock as needed. The resultant purée should be fairly thick.

To decorate for serving, triangles of crisp fried bread may be arranged on top of the purée in a serving dish.

Note: As this purée is likely to stick to the bottom of the pan, keep it warm by placing pan in a roasting tin half-full of hot water in a moderate oven.

The Secret of a really good pea purée: Cook as up to the end of paragraph 2 then add two good tablespoons of fresh cream and a couple of pinches of nutmeg before serving.

LITTLE CASSOULET (BEAN STEW)

Preparation and cooking: 3 hours
In a pressure cooker: 50 minutes

Main course

For 4
500g/1lb white haricot beans
500g/1lb shoulder of mutton (lamb)
50g/2oz ($\frac{1}{4}$ *cup*) goose fat or lard
4 onions
2 cloves garlic
2-3 tomatoes
500g/1lb salt belly pork
Bouquet garni
1 garlic sausage (about 225 - 250g/8oz)
200g/7-8oz salty bacon
250g/8oz pork fat
Breadcrumbs
Salt and pepper

1. Put the beans in a very large saucepan, add cold water to cover and bring to the boil. Allow to boil for 15 minutes (5 minutes in a pressure cooker). Drain, return to the same pan and re-fill with boiling water. Cover and allow to cook for 45 minutes (in a pressure cooker: 15 minutes). Add salt halfway through cooking.
2. Cut the meat into cubes and sauté in the goose fat or lard. Chop the onions and garlic, add to the meat with the skinned tomatoes, with the seeds removed, the belly pork, cut in pieces, the bouquet garni, pepper and a little salt.
3. Drain the beans well. Replace in the pan with the meat and all the other ingredients, adding the garlic sausage, bacon and pork fat, chopped. Allow to simmer together for $1\frac{1}{2}$ hours (in a pressure cooker: 30 minutes).
4. Turn the stew into a large gratin dish, sprinkle thickly with breadcrumbs and brown quickly under the grill (broiler).

The Secret of soft and tender beans: The salt, like the tomatoes, is added halfway through cooking the beans. If added at the start, it toughens the skins and hinders the cooking.

PIGS' TAILS WITH LENTILS

Preparation and cooking: 1½ hours Main course
In a pressure cooker: 20 minutes

For 4
4 pigs' tails
400g/1 lb lentils
1 onion
1 clove
1 carrot
1 clove garlic
Bouquet garni
Salt and pepper

1. In a large saucepan or pressure cooker put the pigs' tails cut in pieces, the peeled onion stuck with a clove, the peeled carrot, clove of garlic, bouquet garni, salt and pepper. Cover completely with cold water and bring to the boil.
2. Put the lentils into a large pan of cold water, boil for 5 minutes and drain. Add them to the saucepan and simmer with the pigs' tails for 1 hour (in a pressure cooker: 20 minutes).

The Secret of well-cooked lentils which do not reduce to a purée: They should simmer very gently and not bubble during the cooking time. Note that small green lentils cook a bit faster than other types.

DESSERTS

Nowadays, many people prefer to end the meal with cheese and fresh fruit, especially if cooking at home. However, Françoise Bernard's puddings are not of the heavy gâteau and cream variety, but use meringue and fresh fruit, in particular pineapple and bananas. There's a traditional cream caramel and a French chocolate semolina for those who like a smooth finish to a delicious meal.

MERINGUES

Preparation and cooking: 1½ hours

For 4
2 egg whites
8 (*10*) tablespoons sugar
1 tablespoon lemon juice
A little flour
A pinch of salt

1. Put the egg whites, sugar, salt and lemon juice into a bowl. Beat with an electric beater until you have a very smooth, glossy cream which sticks to the blades of the whisk.
2. Sprinkle a baking tray with flour and place tablespoonfuls of the meringue mixture on it, well spaced-out. Cook (or rather dry out) in a cool oven (Gas Mark ½–1, 250 – 275°F, 140°C) for about 1 hour, until the meringues are lightly-browned and dry.

The Secret of successful meringues: It lies in the cooking. Meringue browns very quickly and you think it is cooked, but on taking it out of the oven, the centre is still soft. Remember that meringues should *dry out* rather than cook. (Professional pastry-cooks leave them overnight in the warmth of the oven.)

CHANTILLY CREAM

Preparation: 10 minutes

For 4
250g/½ pint (1¼ *cups*) thick cream
A little cold milk, or water
1 tablespoon vanilla-flavoured sugar
An ice cube, if possible

1. Into a deep bowl, pour the fresh cream, and add a little *very cold* milk to dilute. Whisk with an electric blender on a slow speed to incorporate as much air as possible into the cream.
2. Stop whisking immediately the cream thickens and begins to stick to the beaters, or it will get too thick, and 'turn'. Fold in the vanilla-flavoured sugar, without beating.

Trick: Add an ice cube if the cream shows signs of becoming too thick, or 'turning'.

Note: Vanilla-flavoured sugar, so often used in French cooking to flavour cakes and custards, can be made by simply placing a vanilla pod (bean) in a jar of fine sugar. With a well-fitting lid, the flavour of the bean will permeate the sugar.

The Secret of perfect Chantilly cream: It depends on the freshness of the cream, on its being as cold as possible and of a fairly fluid consistency. If necessary, add a little very cold milk, or water, or an ice cube.

SOUFFLÉ OMELETTE

Preparation and cooking: ½ hour

For 4
5 eggs, separated
5 tablespoons caster (fine) sugar
Grated lemon or orange rind (to taste)
30g/1¼oz (*2 Tbsp*) butter or margarine
A pinch of salt

1. Set the oven at Gas Mark 4, 350°F, 180°C. Beat the egg yolks, sugar and grated lemon or orange rind vigorously with a fork, until the mixture lightens in colour.
2. Add a pinch of salt to the egg whites and whisk them so they hold firm peaks, then fold them into the yolk mixture.
3. On top of the stove, heat (but do not brown) the butter or margarine in a large, thick-bottomed ovenproof pan. Pour in the omelette mixture, and stir continuously over a moderate heat.
4. When the omelette begins to 'set' underneath, slip the pan into the pre-set oven for 12 minutes. Serve the omelette folded in half on a rectangular plate.

The Secret of a good soufflé omelette: Once the whisked egg whites have been folded into the yolk mixture, you must work fast. The whites can quickly collapse and turn to liquid. Start cooking as quickly as possible.

'SNOWBALLS'

Preparation and cooking: 45 minutes + cooling time

For 4
½ litre/¾ pint (2½ *cups*) milk
4–5 (*5–6*) tablespoons sugar
1 vanilla pod (bean) or a little vanilla-flavoured sugar (see previous recipe)
4 eggs, separated
A pinch of salt

1. Make a *'Crème Anglaise'* (English cream). In a pan, boil the milk with the sugar, salt and vanilla pod (if using, or add the vanilla sugar). Pour a little boiling milk over the egg yolks in a bowl and stir vigorously. Then pour this mixture back into the pan, stirring continuously, over a low heat until the cream begins to thicken. Do not allow to boil. Set aside to chill in the refrigerator.
2. Make the 'snowballs'. Put a large saucepan of water on to boil. Whisk the egg whites until the mixture holds firm peaks. When water is on the point of boiling, drop in 4 or 5 tablespoonfuls of egg white to form snowballs (*a*). Don't cook more at one time or they will stick together. Leave to cook for a few seconds then turn them over immediately with the spoon (*b*). After a few more seconds, when they are nicely puffed out, take out with a draining spoon, and drain on absorbent paper. Cook the rest of the whisked egg white in the same way.
3. When ready to serve, place the cooled 'snowballs' on top of the well-chilled cream.

A. Using a tablespoon, drop 4–5 'snowballs' into the barely boiling water.
B. Turn them gently, in rotation, almost immediately.

The Secrets of perfect 'snowballs': If you are worried about the crème Anglaise curdling, stir a teaspoon of flour into the cold milk before boiling it.

For light, fluffy, white 'snowballs' cook them very fast in *water* (some recipes suggest using milk – this tends to discolour them and they stick to the pan).

Don't put snowballs on top of the chilled cream until you are about to serve it. They can be made several hours in advance but must be kept separately in the refrigerator.

BANANA OMELETTES

Preparation and cooking: $\frac{1}{4}$ hour

For 4
6 eggs
2 firm bananas
40g/1$\frac{1}{2}$oz (*3 Tbsp*) butter or margarine
2–3 scant tablespoons sugar
2 liqueur glasses rum
A pinch of salt

1. Peel and cut the bananas into medium-size rings; sauté them quickly in a little butter or margarine for 2–3 minutes over a high heat.
2. Melt the rest of the butter or margarine in a large frypan or skillet. Beat the eggs, add a pinch of salt then pour into pan, continuing to beat them lightly. Cook the omelette in the very hot pan over high heat. Before folding the omelette over, arrange the sautéed bananas down one side. Fold the unfilled half over the bananas and place omelette on an oblong dish and sprinkle well with sugar. Heat the rum in a saucepan and, when boiling, set it alight. Pour it, still flaming, over the omelette and serve immediately.

The Secret of a filled omelette which does not stick: The filling, in this case bananas, must not be cooked in the same pan as the omelette. The omelette pan or skillet must be perfectly clean, or the eggs will stick.

PINEAPPLE RICE WITH MERINGUE

Preparation and cooking: 1 hour

For 6
1 large can pineapple cubes (538g/1lb 3oz)
2 tablespoons rum
2 eggs plus 1 or 2 egg whites
2 scant tablespoons caster (fine) sugar
A pinch of salt

The creamed rice
200g/7oz (1¼ cups) Carolina rice
¾ litre/1½ pints (3¾ cups) milk
25g/1oz (*2 Tbsp*) butter
1 tablespoon vanilla-flavoured sugar (*see page 202*)
5 (6) tablespoons caster (fine) sugar
2 pinches of salt

1. Drain the pineapple pieces and soak in the rum while cooking the creamed rice.
2. *The creamed rice.* Wash the rice. Boil for 5 minutes in plenty of water. Drain and turn into a large, thick based pan with the milk, butter and 2 pinches of salt. Partly cover and leave to simmer until the milk is completely absorbed (35 to 40 minutes). After about 20 minutes, add the sugar and vanilla-flavoured sugar.
3. Separate the eggs and add the yolks to the rice, beating them in quickly with a wooden spoon so as not to cook them. Turn out into a deep flameproof dish. Now cover with the pineapple pieces. Whisk the egg whites until they are firm and fluffy, and immediately add 2 scant tablespoons of sugar. Spread this meringue mixture over the pineapple rice. Slide under the grill (broiler) or place in a very hot oven (Gas Mark 8–9, 450 – 475°F, 240°C) to lightly brown the meringue. Serve warm. This dessert can also be served in individual dishes.

The Secret of meringue which does not shrink: Make sure that the meringue mixture is spread thoroughly over the entire pineapple rice so that it sticks firmly to the rim of the cooking dish.

PINEAPPLE GÂTEAU

Preparation and cooking: 1 hour

For 4
1 small can pineapple rings (at least 283g/10oz)
2 tablespoons sugar
A few glacé cherries (optional)

The batter
2 eggs
100g/4oz ($\frac{1}{2}$ *cup*) butter or margarine
100g/4oz (*generous $\frac{1}{2}$ cup*) caster (fine) sugar
100g/4oz (*scant cup*) flour
1 heaped teaspoon of powdered yeast
2 pinches of salt

1 round shallow mould about 20 cm (8 in) diameter

1. Grease the inside of the mould. Sprinkle it with 2 tablespoons of sugar. Line the bottom of the mould with halved, drained pineapple rings.
2. *The batter*: Cream together the softened butter or margarine and sugar in a bowl. Gradually add the eggs, flour, yeast and pinches of salt. Pour this mixture over the fruit. Cook in a moderate oven (Gas Mark 5–6, 375–400°F, 190–200°C.) for 35 to 40 minutes. As soon as it is cooked, remove from the baking mould. The pineapple topping may be decorated with glacé cherries.

The Secret of a yeast-based gâteau which rises well: Cooking should begin in a moderate oven so that the heat reaches the heart of the cake before the outside begins to brown. If the outside cooks first, it effectively seals the batter and stops it from rising.

BANANA PANCAKES FLAMBÉ

Preparation and cooking: 45 minutes
Mixture to stand: 30 minutes

For 8 large pancakes
150g/6oz (1½ *cups*) flour
¼ teaspoon salt
2 eggs
2 large glasses milk or water
1 tablespoon oil

4 bananas
30g/1¼oz (*2 Tbsp*) butter or margarine
2–3 liqueur glasses rum
Caster (fine) sugar for sprinkling

1. *The pancakes*: Put the flour, salt, eggs, milk or water and oil in a mixing bowl. Beat with an electric mixer until a smooth, liquidy dough is formed. Allow to stand in a cool place for at least 30 minutes, if possible.
2. Dip a piece of absorbent kitchen paper in oil and keep it to rub over the inside of the frypan or skillet between cooking each pancake. Put the pan over a high heat. When it is very hot, pour in a small quantity of pancake mixture. Tilt the pan from side to side so that the mixture spreads thinly and evenly over the entire base and when the edges look dry and start to brown, flip the pancake over and cook the other side. Sugar each pancake as it is cooked.
3. Slice the bananas in two lengthways. Brown them quickly on both sides in a pan with the butter or margarine.
4. Place one in each pancake and roll up and place them on a long metal serving tray. Sprinkle with sugar and keep hot. Just before serving, pour the rum into a small pan, bring to the boil and set alight. Pour quickly over the warm pancakes and serve.

The Secret of rum which flames properly: The rum *must* be boiling hot. Light with a match and it should flare up at once (don't be afraid; it won't burn).

PINEAPPLE PANCAKES

Preparation and cooking: ¾ hour
Mixture to stand: ½ hour

For 8 pancakes
100g/4oz (*1 cup*) flour
2 cups milk
2 eggs
Salt

1 can creamed rice (440g/16oz)
1 small can pineapple rings (at least 283/10oz)
8 glacé cherries
½ wineglass rum

1. *The pancakes.* Put all the pancake ingredients into a mixing bowl and beat with an electric mixer until a smooth, liquid dough is formed. Leave to stand for at least 30 minutes. Fry each pancake in a very hot pan over high heat (see previous recipe), wiping out the pan between each with a strip of absorbent paper dipped in oil. Stack the cooked pancakes with a piece of waxed or greaseproof paper between each one and keep hot in a moderate oven (Gas Mark 4, 350°F, 175°C).
2. Slowly heat the rice through with a little pineapple juice. Put one level tablespoon of creamed rice on each pancake, roll up, arrange them side by side on an ovenproof plate and keep them hot.
3. Just before serving, decorate each pancake with a half-slice of pineapple and a glacé cherry. Heat the rum in a small pan to boiling point, quickly pour over the warm pancakes and set alight. Serve immediately.

The Secret of pancakes which do not stick: The longer you leave the mixture in a cool place before cooking, the less risk there is of the pancakes sticking to the pan. The mixture can be left for up to 12 hours in a refrigerator without harm.

CREAM CARAMEL

Preparation and cooking: 45 minutes
Chill for: 2 hours

For 4
½ litre/1 pint *(2½ cups)* milk
6 tablespoons sugar
1 teaspoon vanilla-flavoured sugar (or 1 vanilla bean)
3–4 eggs
A pinch of salt

The caramel sauce
3–4 tablespoons sugar
2–3 tablespoons water
A few drops of lemon juice

6-inch diameter (1½ pint capacity) mould

1. *The caramel sauce*: Bring to the boil the sugar, water and a few drops of lemon juice in a pan. Allow the caramel to boil rapidly, without stirring, until it starts to turn brown, then remove the pan from the heat. Pour the caramel carefully into a mould and tilt the mould so that the liquid caramel coats the sides evenly. Allow to cool.

2. *The cream*: Put the measured milk with a pinch of salt, the sugar and vanilla sugar (or bean, if using) in a pan and bring to the boil. Beat the eggs in a bowl and, still stirring, add a little of the hot milk. Take out the vanilla pod, then pour this mixture back into the pan, stirring continuously. Pour the custard through a fine sieve into the caramel-lined mould. Put into a bain-marie (see below) in a fairly hot oven (Gas Mark 5, 375°F, 190°C) for 25–30 minutes. Leave to cool completely before turning out of the mould.

Note: For a 'bain-marie', take a large cooking tin, half-fill with hot water, and carefully lift the mould into the centre. Place the tin in the oven and cook for the appropriate time.

The Secret of perfectly smooth cream caramel: Before cooking, pass the beaten eggs and boiling milk through a very fine sieve. The sieve retains any particles of egg which might coagulate in cooking and spoil the smoothness.

PEARS IN RED WINE

Preparation and cooking: ½ hour

For 6
8 small pears
½ litre/1 pint (2½ *cups*) red wine
8 level tablespoons caster (fine) sugar
1 tablespoon vanilla-flavoured sugar (*see page 202*)

Peel the pears, keeping them whole. Heat the red wine with the sugar and vanilla sugar. When this starts to bubble, put in the pears and leave them to cook gently for 15–25 minutes, until they look transparent, and are thoroughly cooked. Leave them to cool in the syrup.

Variation: If you just want pears in syrup, omit the red wine and add the equivalent quantity of cold water.

CHOCOLATE SEMOLINA

Preparation and cooking: 20 minutes
Cooling time: 1 hour

For 4
½ litre/1 pint (2½ *cups*) milk
50g/2 oz (*4 Tbsp*) sugar
50g/2 oz (*4 Tbsp*) butter
50g/2oz (*2 squares*) semi-sweet chocolate
60g/2½oz (⅓ *cup*) fine semolina
A pinch of salt

1–2 pint capacity deep-sided jelly mould

1. Put the milk, sugar, salt, butter and chocolate into a pan. Bring slowly to the boil. Sprinkle the semolina into the pan and stir vigorously with a wooden spoon. Leave to cook gently for 10 minutes.
2. Immerse a deep-sided jelly mould in cold water, drain, then pour the mixture into the wet mould. Leave until completely set before turning out.

Organization: Make enough for two servings by simply doubling the quantities of ingredients and turn out into two moulds. The second dessert can be kept in a refrigerator for up to three days.

The Secret of a deliciously smooth semolina pudding: To prevent lumps forming, it is important to keep to the exact proportions of semolina-to-liquid, indicated in the recipe. Keep the cooking time to exactly 10 minutes.

RECIPE INDEX

KEY: MC Main Course, HS Hot Starter, CS Cold Starter, D Dessert, SD Side Dish, PD Party Dish, SS Side Salad, * Secret

BEEF 39–51
Bourguignon MC * 46
Fillet of, Portugaise MC * 49
Fondue Bourguignonne MC * 47
French Roast MC 39
Pot Roast MC 40, * 41
Spit Roast MC 40
Steak, Entrecôte, Bordelaise MC * 45
Steak, Grilled (Broiled) MC * 42
Steak, Peppered MC * 44
Stew, Béarnaise MC * 50
Vigneronne MC 51

CROUTONS 4, 93

DESSERTS 199–214
Banana Omelettes D * 206
Banana Pancakes Flambé D * 209
Chantilly Cream D * 202
Chocolate Semolina D * 213
Cream Caramel D * 211
Meringues D * 201
Pears in Red Wine D 212
Pineapple Gâteau D * 208
Pineapple Pancakes D * 210
Pineapple Rice with Meringue D * 207
'Snowballs' D * 203

EGGS
Banana Omelettes D * 206
Cream Caramel D * 211
en Cocotte Roquefort HS/CS * 32
Fillings for Hard-Boiled Eggs CS/MC * 34
Omelette HS/MC * 36
Portuguese Egg Timbale HS/MC * 33
Soufflé Omelette D * 204

FISH AND SHELLFISH 137–151
Fish
Cod with Russian Salad MC * 141
Court-bouillon for, * 139
Lotte 'ew Matelot' MC * 149
Mackerel with Garlic MC * 143
Paupiettes in Cream MC * 146
Quenelles (Fish Creams) HS * 13
Red Mullet 'en Papillote' MC/HS * 144
Red Mullet with Herbs MC * 145
Salmon in Aspic PD * 151
Salmon with Mousseline Sauce MC * 150
Sole, Stuffed Fillet of MC * 142
Trout in White Wine MC * 147
Trout with Chives MC * 148
White Fish Soup HS * 4

Shellfish
Avocadoes, Stuffed with CS * 28
Crab, with Grapefruit CS * 29
Crab Matatou MC * 153
Lobster à l'Américaine MC * 160
Lobster, Baked MC/HS * 159
Moules Marinière HS * 19
Musse! Quiche HS * 20
Oyster Cocktail CS * 18
Prawn Fritters HS * 17
Scallops in Cream Sauce MC * 156
Scallops in Pastry Shells MC * 154
Scallops St Jacques Mornay MC * 157
Scampi, Floating HS/CS * 15
Scampi à la Crème HS 16
Scampi Valencienne MC * 162
Shellfish, Stuffed MC * 158

FRUIT
Avocado and Grapefruit Salad CS/SS * 26
Banana Omelettes D * 206
Banana Pancakes Flambé D * 209
Grapefruit with Crab CS * 29
Pears in Red Wine D 212
Pineapple Gâteau D * 208
Pineapple Pancakes D * 210
Pineapple Rice with Meringue D * 207

HAM
Cornets HS * 10
with Cream and Port HS * 12

LAMB AND MUTTON
Blanquette MC * 81
Breast, with Spinach Stuffing MC * 78
Cassoulet, Little (Bean Stew) MC * 197
Cutlets Champvallon MC * 79
Cutlets Milanaise MC * 80
Dolmas MC * 84
Leg of Lamb Boulangère MC * 82
Leg, Roast MC * 76
Moussaka MC * 83
Shoulder, Braised with Herb Stuffing MC * 77
Windsor Pie MC * 85

MAIN COURSE DISHES 37–62
Fish and Shellfish 137–162
Meat 38–100
Poultry and Game 101–135

MARINADES for Meat and Game, 87

MAYONNAISE 21, 29

OFFAL (Variety Meats)
Brains Meunière MC * 97
Chicken Liver Terrine CS * 6
Kidneys Baugé MC * 93
Kidneys, Maître d'Hôtel MC * 96
Kidneys in Mustard MC * 94
Kidneys in Port Wine MC * 95
Liver and Onions MC * 92
Liver en Meurette MC * 90
Liver with Anchovy MC * 89
Sweetbreads en Cocotte MC * 98
Tripe Alger MC * 99
Tripe au Gratin MC * 100

PASTA AND RICE
Gnocchi Romana SD/HS * 170
Macaroni Languedoc SD/HS * 169
Macaroni Ring Salad CS/SS * 21
Noodles, Roquefort SD/HS * 168
Pasta, Home-made SD * 165
Rice, Plain Boiled SD * 172
Rice, Sautéed SD 174
Rice Pilaf SD * 173
Risotto with Olives MC * 175
Semolina, Chocolate D * 213
Semolina, Italian SD * 171

PÂTÉ
Breton Pâtés (Individual) HS * 5

Chicken Liver Terrine CS * 6
Rabbit Terrine CS * 9
Turkey Terrine CS * 8

PORK 53–61
and Veal Pie MC/HS/CS * 60
Braised MC * 56
Braised, with Orange MC * 57
Chops 'en Saupiquet' MC * 53
Country Stew Limousine MC * 59
Cutlets, Stuffed MC * 54
Escalopes in Red Wine MC * 61
Goulash MC * 58
Paupiettes with Fennel MC * 55
Pigs' Tails with Lentils MC * 198
POULTRY AND GAME 6–9, 101–135
Chicken
Cold, in Aspic MC * 109
Coq au Vin MC * 111
Fowl-in-the Pot MC * 110
Liver Terrine CS * 6
Martinique MC * 113
Oven Roast MC 103
Provençal MC 114
Sauté Vallée d'Auge MC * 112
Spit Roast MC * 104
Duck
Normandy MC * 125
Roast MC * 123
with Orange MC * 124
Goose
Braised MC * 120
Curried MC * 121
Stuffed with Chestnuts MC * 122
Hare
Jugged MC * 135
Partridge
on Canapés MC * 126
Pigeon
Grand-Mère MC * 128
Stuffed Toulouse MC * 129
Quail
with Grapes MC * 127
Rabbit
Flemish MC * 131
Stew (Blanquette of Rabbit) MC * 133
Terrine CS * 9
with Mustard and Cream Sauce MC * 132
with Shallots MC * 130
Turkey
Braised MC * 120
Brochettes MC * 119
Curried MC * 121
Terrine CS * 8
with Mushroom Stuffing MC * 115

SALADS
Avocado and Grapefruit CS/SS * 26
Macaroni Ring CS/SS * 21
Russian SS 141

SAUCES
FOR Fondue Bourgignonne 48
for Pasta 166
for Steaks * 43
Tomato 32, 92, 100, 167

SOUPS 3-4
Cheese and Onion Soup with Port Wine HS * 3
White Fish Soup HS * 4

STARTERS (Appetizers)
Artichokes and Pink Sauce CS * 22
Asparagus Milanaise HS * 23
Aubergines, Stuffed HS * 24
Avocado and Grapefruit Salad CS/SS * 26
Avocadoes, Stuffed CS * 27, 28
Breton Pâtés (Individual) HS * 5
Cheese and Onion Soup with Port Wine HS * 3
Chicken Liver Terrine CS * 6
Eggs en Cocotte Roquefort HS/CS * 32
Egg Timbale, Portuguese HS/MC * 33
Fillings for Hard-Boiled Eggs CS/MC * 34
Gnocchi Romana SD/HS * 170
Grapefruit with Crab CS * 29
Ham Cornets HS * 10
Ham with Cream and Port Wine HS * 12
Lobster, Baked MC/HS * 159
Macaroni Languedoc SD/HS * 169
Macaroni Ring Salad CS/SS * 21
Moules Marinière HS * 19
Mussel Quiche HS * 20
Omelette HS/MC * 36
Oyster Cocktail CS * 18
Prawn Fritters HS * 17
Quenelles HS * 13
Rabbit Terrine CS * 9
Red Mullet 'en Papillote' MC/HS * 144
Roquefort Noodles SD/HS * 169
Scampi, Floating HS/CS 15
Scampi à la Crème HS 16
Tomato Quiche HS/MC * 31
Tomatoes, Stuffed HS * 30
Turkey Terrine CS * 8
Veal and Pork Pie MC/HS/CS * 60
White Fish Soup HS * 4

STUFFINGS
for Chicken, 106-8
for Turkey, 117-18

VEAL
and Pork Pie MC/HS/CS * 60
Blanquette à l'Ancienne MC * 72
Breast of, Paysanne MC * 71
Chops Vallée d'Auge MC * 69
Cutlets 'en Papillote' MC * 66
Cutlets Normande MC * 70
Escalopes in Breadcrumbs MC * 64
Escalopes with Orange MC * 65
Marengo MC * 74
Pâtés, Breton (Individual) HS * 5
Paupiettes Cordon Bleu MC * 67
Paupiettes Provençal MC * 68
Sauté Mentonnaise MC * 73
Spit-Roast MC * 63

VEGETABLES
Artichokes and Pink Sauce CS * 22
Asparagus Milanaise HS * 23
Aubergines, Stuffed HS * 24
Avocado and Grapefruit Salad CS/SS * 26
Avocadoes, Stuffed CS * 27, 28
Bean Stew (Little Cassoulet) MC * 197
Beetroot in Cream Sauce V * 185
Carrots à la Crème V * 187
Carrots Pompadour V 188
Cassoulet (Bean Stew) MC * 197
Cauliflower, Creamed V * 189
Chick Pea Salad V * 195
Courgettes Lyonnaise V 190
Dolmas MC * 84
Lentils (with Pigs' Tails) MC * 198
Onions, Glazed V * 192
Potato Croquettes V * 184
Potatoes, Dauphinois V * 180
Potatoes, Domino V 182
Potato Galette V * 183
Purée St Germain V * 196
Ratatouille Cordon Bleu V * 193
Red Cabbage Bernoise V * 186
Rösti (Swiss Potatoes) V * 179
Runner Beans, Venetian-Style V 191
Tomato Quiche, Savoury HS/MC * 31
Tomatoes, Stuffed HS * 30
Turnips in Cider, Stuffed V 194

VARIETY MEATS, see **OFFAL**